Also by Doreen Rappaport

LIVING DANGEROUSLY
American Women Who Risked Their Lives for Adventure

ESCAPE FROM SLAVERY
Five Journeys to Freedom

AMERICAN WOMEN
Their Lives in Their Words

THE BOSTON COFFEE PARTY

TROUBLE AT THE MINES

Be the Judge **?** Be the Jury
THE LIZZIE BORDEN TRIAL

BE THE JUDGE? BE THE JURY™
THE SACCO-VANZETTI TRIAL
DOREEN RAPPAPORT

ILLUSTRATED WITH
PHOTOGRAPHS, PRINTS,
AND DIAGRAMS

HarperCollins*Publishers*

Reprinted with permission of *The Boston Herald*: 11, April 16, 1920; 18, May 7, 1920; 29, June 5, 1921; 46, June 10, 1921; 64, June 18, 1921; 73, June 22, 1921; 79, June 23, 1921; 90, June 28, 1921; 107, 112, July 6, 1921; 117, July 7, 1921; 143, July 13, 1921; 164, August 23, 1927. By courtesy of the Trustees of the Boston Public Library: 12, 13, 25, 44, 49, 56, 71, 80, 94, 103, 106, 115, 137, 143, 163.

The Sacco-Vanzetti Trial

Library of Congress Cataloging-in-Publication Data
Rappaport, Doreen.
    The Sacco-Vanzetti trial / Doreen Rappaport ; illustrated with photographs, prints, and diagrams.
        p.   cm. — (Be the judge / be the jury)
    Includes bibliographical references and index.
    Summary: Recreates the murder trial of Italian immigrants Sacco and Vanzetti, using edited transcripts of the testimony given in the case, and invites the reader to act as judge and jury.
    ISBN 0-06-025115-8. — ISBN 0-06-025116-6 (lib. bdg.)
    1. Sacco-Vanzetti case—Juvenile literature.   2. Trials (Murder)—Massachusetts—Dedham—Juvenile literature.   [1. Sacco-Vanzetti case. 2. Trials (Murder).]   I. Title.   II. Series: Rappaport, Doreen. Be the judge-be the jury.
KF224.S2R36   1992   91-47509
345.73'02523—dc20   CIP
[347.3052523]   AC

1   2   3   4   5   6   7   8   9   10   ❖
First Edition
Diagrams by Meera Kothari
Logo Icons by Chris Cart

For Laurel and Gene Eisner,
for their unflagging commitment
to social justice and friendship

Contents

Scene of the Crime

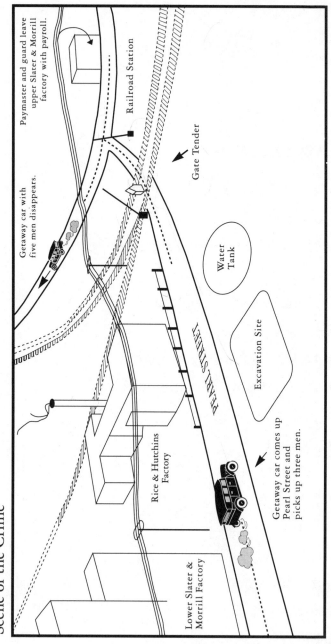

Paymaster and guard leave upper Slater & Morrill factory with payroll.

Railroad Station

Gate Tender

Getaway car with five men disappears.

Water Tank

Excavation Site

PEARL STREET

Rice & Hutchins Factory

Lower Slater & Morrill Factory

Getaway car comes up Pearl Street and picks up three men.

Everything in this book really happened. This book contains the actual testimony of the witnesses at the Sacco-Vanzetti trial.

Before the Trial

The Crime

On April 15, 1920, in South Braintree, Massachusetts, two men shot and killed a paymaster and his guard who were carrying the weekly payroll of a shoe company.

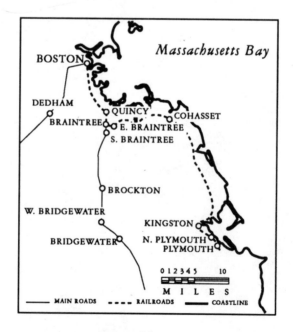

The gunmen seized the metal boxes and escaped with three other men in a stolen car. Three weeks later Nicola Sacco and Bartolomeo Vanzetti were arrested for the murders. Thirteen months after that their trial began. It became headline news as people all over the world argued whether these men were guilty or innocent.

> ## MOTOR BANDITS MURDER GUARD, WOUND PAYMASTER, DASH AWAY WITH $18,000

Headline from *The Boston Herald*

For as long as it takes you to read this book, you will BE THE JURY at Sacco and Vanzetti's trial. You will sit in the jury box and listen to witnesses testify and be cross-examined. You will hear the evidence and decide whether or not Sacco and Vanzetti are guilty or not guilty of first-degree murder.

You will also have a chance to BE THE JUDGE and make rulings that affect the defendants' lives.

Read carefully. Think carefully about everything you read. Do not make your decision lightly, for you hold Sacco's and Vanzetti's lives in your hands.

Who Was Nicola Sacco?

In 1908, seventeen-year-old Sacco left Italy and emigrated to the United States. For four years he worked as a water boy, steamroller oiler, and slag shoveler. In 1912 he became an edge trimmer in a shoe factory and for a while earned $40 a week—good money in those days. In April 1920 he had a job in a shoe factory near the scene of the crime. At that time he was married and had a two-year-old son, Dante; his wife, Rosina, was pregnant. Sacco and his wife were aliens (non-citizens).

Who Was Bartolomeo Vanzetti?

In 1908, twenty-year-old Vanzetti emigrated to the United States from Italy. He arrived in New York and found it hard to get a job. He did not speak English. He worked as a dishwasher, ditch digger, farmer, assistant pastry chef, and ice cutter. In 1913 he settled in Plymouth, Massachusetts. At the time of the robbery, Vanzetti sold fish from a cart. When the fish business wasn't good, he took whatever jobs he could get. Vanzetti was an alien, though he had begun the process for citizenship.

How Did Other Americans Feel About Immigrants in 1920?

Italians formed the largest group of immigrants arriving in the States at the turn of the century. Many wealthy Protestant Americans believed that southern Italians, who were mostly peasants, were inferior. Sacco and Vanzetti were from southern Italy.

Many people who were prejudiced against new immigrants were also against unions, for it was the new immigrants, wanting better pay, who organized unions. The unions often set up strikes which encouraged workers to stop working in order to get what they wanted—better pay and better working conditions. But the strikes angered business people who did not want to pay their workers more. The leaders of the unions were labeled "radicals" to suggest that their ideas and actions were extreme and unnecessary.

Radical labor leaders were arrested and put in prison for a long time. Federal laws banned radical literature from the mail. The government drew up lists of "undesirables" whose political ideas were considered dangerous. But the strikes and protests did not stop.

The success of the Russian Revolution in 1917 whipped antiradical feelings in the United States into a fury. Many recent immigrants were radical in their thinking. They were anarchists, communists, and socialists. These philosophies were different, but people often lumped them together and labeled them all as "Reds" or "communists."

Laws were passed to get rid of these "radicals" or "Reds." The Immigration Act of 1903 banned immigrants who believed in or urged the overthrow of the government; such people could be deported. The Immigration Act of 1917 banned people who taught others to "unlawfully destroy property."

On January 2, 1920, United States Attorney General Michael Palmer launched a series of raids. Over 4,000 people in thirty-three cities were arrested. People were hauled out of their beds and seized in meeting halls, restaurants, and schools. Homes were smashed as police searched for books and papers to prove that these people were "communists." Aliens in towns in Massachusetts were arrested, along with American citizens. Most arrests and most of the searches were done illegally.

Trials and deportations began, and so did bombings of some public officials who had worked against the radicals. Massachusetts had its share of bombings and strikes.

Why Were Sacco and Vanzetti Considered "Undesirables"?

Sacco and Vanzetti were part of a group of anarchists who believed that society needed to be changed. They believed that the U.S. government had to be overthrown before there could be true equality and justice in the country. At the time of the robbery their group was being investigated by the federal government. Both men knew aliens who were being deported. One of their friends, Andrew Salsedo, had been arrested in New York City and had supposedly jumped from a jail window to his death.

How Did Sacco and Vanzetti Get to Trial?
Investigation: April 15, 1920

The police questioned people near the scene of the crime. Most eyewitnesses thought the gunmen were Italians. Two days later the getaway car was found stripped of license plates. It was dusted for prints, but none were found.

Four months earlier, on December 24, 1919, there had been an unsuccessful robbery attempt in Bridgewater, a town 18 miles from South Braintree. The police thought two Italian anarchists named Feruccio Coacci and Michael Boda might have been involved in one or both robberies. They could not find Coacci to question him. Boda was questioned once and then disappeared.

The Arrest: May 5, 1920

On May 5, the police found out that Boda and three other men—Sacco, Vanzetti, and Riccardo Orciani—had gone to a garage to pick up Boda's car. The police set out after them. Sacco and Vanzetti were arrested and charged with carrying concealed weapons./ In the next few days witnesses from the South Braintree rob-

Headline from *The Boston Herald*

bery and murder identified both men. Five witnesses from the Bridgewater robbery identified Vanzetti as one of the gunmen. Orciani was picked up and had an alibi for both robberies. Boda was never found.

The prosecutor thought he had enough evidence to bring both men to trial for the South Braintree murders and to bring Vanzetti to trial for attempted robbery and intent to murder in the Bridgewater crime. On July 1 a jury convicted Vanzetti of both charges in the Bridgewater crime.

Preliminary Hearing: May 26, 1920

For some unexplained reason, the preliminary

hearing involved only Sacco. There is no record of Vanzetti having a hearing. The police testified about what they had learned. Eyewitnesses testified. The judge decided that there was *probable cause*, or reasonable grounds for believing that Sacco committed the crime.

Grand Jury: September 11, 1920

A grand jury of twenty-three men was selected from voter registration roles. (Women did not yet have the right to vote.) Because defendants and their lawyers are not allowed to attend grand jury proceedings, the grand jury heard only prosecution witnesses and then the prosecution's summary of the case. The grand jury decided that there was enough evidence to bring the two men to trial. It issued an indictment charging them with first-degree murder. First-degree murder is generally a killing that has been *premeditated* (thought out beforehand). The penalty for first-degree murder was death.

The Arraignment: September 28, 1920

The defendants entered a formal plea of "not guilty" to the charges.

What Are the Rights of Accused Murderers Under the Constitution?

Fourth Amendment. Without permission or a search warrant, their homes cannot be searched and articles in their homes cannot be taken.

Fifth Amendment. The defendants must be charged by a grand jury. If the grand jury decides there is enough evidence to bring them to trial, it issues an indictment. Sacco and Vanzetti cannot be forced to testify against themselves. They cannot be convicted without *due process* under the law: Fair legal procedures must be followed.

Sixth Amendment. They must have a speedy and public trial with an impartial jury. They must be informed of all charges against them. They must be able to cross-examine witnesses against them and have time to present witnesses in their favor. They have a right to have a lawyer represent them.

Eighth Amendment. There may be no excessively high bail or fines or "cruel and unusual punishment."

What Is a Trial?

A trial is like a contest between two opponents: The prosecutor represents the state; the defense lawyer represents the defendants. In a criminal trial, the state brings charges against the defendant. The prosecutor tries to convince the jury that the defendant is guilty of the charges beyond a reasonable doubt. The defense lawyer tries to disprove the charges and show that there is reasonable doubt that the defendant is guilty.

The official name for this trial is *The Commonwealth of Massachusetts versus Nicola Sacco and Bartolomeo Vanzetti*. In the United States a person is considered innocent until proven guilty by a trial—even though a judge has found probable cause and a grand jury has issued an indictment.

What Does the Prosecutor Do?

After reading police reports and questioning witnesses, the prosecutor decided that he had enough evidence to bring both men to trial. He spoke at the preliminary hearing and convinced the judge of probable cause against Sacco. He convinced the grand jury to indict both men. His job at the trial is to prove that they are guilty beyond a reasonable doubt.

What Does the Defense Lawyer Do?

Sacco and Vanzetti were questioned by the police before they had a lawyer. Sacco's lawyer represented him at his preliminary hearing. Once the men were indicted, their lawyers looked for witnesses to establish reasonable doubt of the defendants' guilt and to contradict evidence of prosecution witnesses. At the trial, defense lawyers cross-examine the prosecution's witnesses and try to punch holes in their evidence; later they present their own witnesses.

What Does a Judge Do?

Judges should not take sides. They listen to evidence and make sure a defendant's constitutional rights are protected and that proper procedures are followed. When the lawyers argue over evidence, the judge listens and, based on rules about evidence, decides whether or not the evidence should be admitted.

What Does the Jury Do?

A jury listens to the evidence and decides whether it proves beyond a reasonable doubt that the defendant is guilty. Jury members may not talk about the case with anyone. They are not allowed to read newspaper accounts of the trial. They try to stay impartial or unprejudiced about the case. Sacco and Vanzetti's jury was sequestered: They were not allowed to go home during the six weeks of the trial.

What Does the Defendant Do?

Defendants have the right to be in court every day of the trial, but the Massachusetts Constitution and the Fifth Amendment to the U.S. Constitution state that in criminal cases a defendant does not have to testify. The fact that the defendants might not choose to testify may *not* be interpreted to mean they are guilty.

Sacco's and Vanzetti's presence in court is important. What they wear, how they look, how they carry themselves or act during the trial, affect what the jury thinks of them and may affect its verdict.

Who Took Part in Sacco and Vanzetti's Trial?

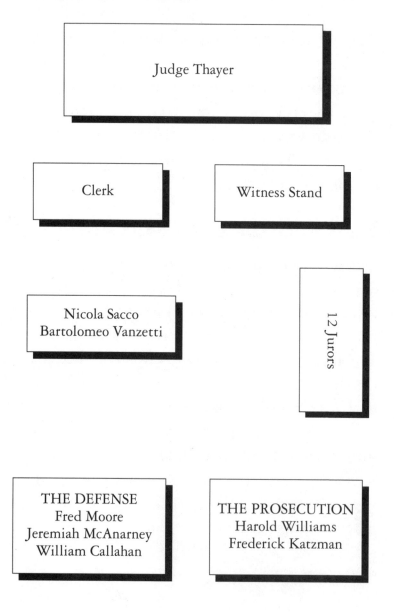

Judge Thayer

Clerk

Witness Stand

Nicola Sacco
Bartolomeo Vanzetti

12 Jurors

THE DEFENSE
Fred Moore
Jeremiah McAnarney
William Callahan

THE PROSECUTION
Harold Williams
Frederick Katzman

Choosing the Jury

Tuesday, May 31, 1921

The Sacco and Vanzetti Defense Committee had launched a publicity campaign to gain support for the men. The authorities, fearing trouble, stepped up police protection. The courthouse was surrounded with state troopers. Some were on horseback, some on motorcycles. Police patrolled the courthouse halls and stairs.

The defense worried that the large number of police would make people believe that their clients were dangerous.

The defendants, who had been in separate jails the past eight months, kissed each other on the cheek when they saw each other. Then they were handcuffed together. Two deputies walked alongside them into the courtroom. They were put in a metal waist-high cage, as was the custom at that time. Their handcuffs were removed. Sacco's wife, Rosina, sat behind her husband, holding their seven-month-old baby on her lap.

Jury selection began. It is hoped that jurors know little or nothing about a case so they can be fair. But this case had been written about so much that both lawyers knew that almost all the jurors would have read something about it. The defense worried that the recent antiradical hysteria and anti-Italian feelings in the country would make it hard to find twelve fair-minded jurors.

To eliminate jurors who were prejudiced, Judge Webster Thayer questioned each man. Among the questions he asked was "Have you formed any opinions that would prevent you from reaching a fair verdict?"

Choosing the jury proved difficult. The men gave reasons not to serve—sick wives, deafness, planned vacations. Some men said they already had made up their minds about the case. The judge became increasingly annoyed as many men asked to be excused because they didn't believe in the death penalty. Many times the prosecutor or the defense asked the judge to excuse a juror because something he said showed that he could not come to a fair verdict. When the judge agreed, he excused the juror. At other times the lawyers asked that a man be excused without a reason. Each lawyer has the right to excuse a certain number of jurors without giving a reason. Fred Moore, Sacco's lawyer, kept objecting to businessmen and more educated men, who he felt would be less sympathetic to the defendants. Jeremiah McAnarney, Vanzetti's lawyer, was worried. He noticed that when the judge spoke to Fred Moore, his eyes and voice showed his dislike.

After ten hours and 175 men questioned, only three jurors had been chosen.

Wednesday, June 1, 1921, to Sunday, June 5, 1921

Some 500 men were rejected for knowing too much about the case or having strong feelings against the death penalty. Deputies were sent throughout the county to get more jurors. Men were awakened from sleep and taken to the courthouse. Some men were summoned as they came home from work. One man was taken from his wedding. Finally, at 1 A.M., on Sunday, June 5, the last juror was sworn in.

SACCO-VANZETTI JURY COMPLETE AFTER 675 TALESMEN ARE CALLED

Largest Murder Trial Panel
Ever Summoned in
Norfolk County

Headline from *The Boston Herald*

Monday, June 6, 1921

There were still great numbers of police outside the courthouse. The defendants, surrounded by police, were led into the courtroom and into the cage, where their handcuffs were taken off. The courtroom was packed with reporters, curious citizens, and people who believed the defendants were innocent.

The clerk read the indictment, listing the charges, and the trial began.

The Prosecution's Opening Statement

In the afternoon, Assistant District Attorney Harold Williams gave his opening statement.

An opening statement reviews the crime and summarizes what the prosecution intends to prove. Prosecutors hope their openings are effective, because they want to impress juries with their side of the case even at this early stage of the trial.

Assistant District Attorney Williams spoke:

The alleged crime took place on April 15, 1920, at 3 P.M. in South Braintree. At 9:35 A.M. Shelly Neal delivered the payroll to the Slater & Morrill upper factory. He noticed the getaway car, a seven-passenger black Buick, in front of the factory. At 3 P.M. paymaster Frederick Parmenter and a guard, Alessandro Berardelli, left the upper factory with two boxes containing the $15,776 payroll to deliver it to the workers in Slater & Morrill's lower factory on Pearl Street. They walked on Pearl Street across the railroad tracks toward the lower factory.

Just past the Rice & Hutchins factory on Pearl Street were two men leaning against the fence. They were short and stocky, about 5 feet and 6 or 7 inches tall. They weighed 140 to 160 pounds. They wore caps and dark clothes. They were apparently Italian.

The two men fired. Berardelli fell wounded. Parmenter dropped his box and ran across the street to an excavation site, where men were working. One bandit followed Parmenter and shot him in the back. The short, swarthy bandit who was shooting Berardelli, lost his cap. That man is identified as Nicola Sacco.

The getaway car appeared. The driver was a light-haired man with a very thin face. A man we can't describe was in the backseat. A third man appeared from somewhere and helped the two shooters pick up the payroll boxes and get into the car. Then they drove toward the railroad crossing. They fired shots from the car.

Gate tender Michael Levangie heard the shots as a train was approaching. He ran to close the gates. The getaway car neared the crossing. A man in the car hollered at Levangie and intimidated him so much that he didn't close the gates. The Buick

Prosecution Eyewitnesses

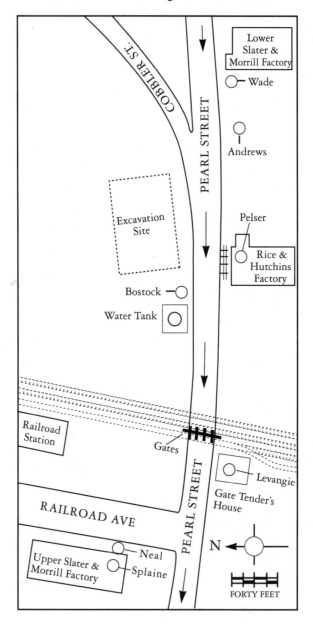

crossed the tracks, and Levangie saw an Italian with a mustache on the front seat. He has identified that man as Bartolomeo Vanzetti.

By now the shots had attracted much attention. People came to the windows of the upper factory. Mary Splaine looked out the factory window right down on that car. She has identified the man shooting out of the car as Sacco.

The car sped away. At Matfield Crossing, the crossing tender, Austin Reed, saw Vanzetti on the front seat. Vanzetti spoke to him.

Now where had this car been since Shelly Neal had seen it in the morning? At 9:20 A.M. John Faulkner saw Vanzetti get off a train at East Braintree. He was picked up there in the Buick and driven to South Braintree. Sometime after 10 A.M. Harry Dolbeare saw the car with Vanzetti in it.

During the police investigation, an officer suspected that a man named Coacci might be one of the robbers. The police went to his house. Coacci wasn't there, but Michael Boda was. The police suspected that the getaway car might have been stored in a shed behind the house. They thought that Boda might have been involved in the robbery, too.

On May 5 the police went after Boda. Three other men—Sacco, Vanzetti, and Riccardo Orciani —were with him. The police arrested the defendants. Sacco had a loaded .32-caliber Colt automatic pistol tucked down inside his pants. He also had twenty-two bullets. Our experts have concluded that the bullet that caused Berardelli's death was fired from a .32 automatic like Sacco's Colt. Vanzetti had a loaded .38-caliber Harrington & Richardson revolver on him. A cap found near Berardelli's body is similar to Sacco's cap. Both men had known each other for some time before this.

We have direct evidence of Sacco shooting at Berardelli. There is no eyewitness evidence that Vanzetti fired any gun. But evidence put Vanzetti in the car and at the scene of the crime. And Massachusetts law says everyone who took part in this holdup and shooting is guilty of murder as much as if they had actually fired the shots.

You will now hear the evidence. I ask for your patience in this long trial ahead.

What Evidence Is Allowed at a Trial?

Each side presents *witnesses* whose testimony tends to support its side of the case. All testimony must reasonably relate to the main issue. Generally, witnesses cannot give their opinions.

Sometimes witnesses give *direct* evidence; they testify about what they have seen or heard ("I saw him shoot the victim"). Sometimes witnesses give *circumstantial* evidence; they testify to the circumstances around the crime, and the jury draws conclusions from these circumstances ("I saw two shadows at the window struggling. Later I went into the room and saw a dead woman").

Expert witnesses are sometimes police officers, medical examiners and ballistics experts (specialists in firearms). Experts may interpret evidence and give their opinions.

Be the Jury

Now listen to the evidence and search for the truth. Remember that even though the defendants have been arrested and charged with murder they are still presumed to be innocent. The prosecutor does *not* have to prove them guilty beyond all *possibility* of a doubt, but the prosecutor must establish their guilt beyond a *reasonable* doubt. The defense does not have to prove their innocence. The defense only needs to point out flaws in evidence to convince the jury to say that guilt was not proven.

What is a *reasonable* doubt? It is a doubt for which some reason can be given. The doubt must come from the evidence or from the lack of evidence. It can come from the fact that there are other solutions to the crime that are just as believable. A doubt is *not* reasonable if it is based on some guess or thought unrelated to the evidence. A doubt can *not* be based merely on sympathy for the defendants or belief that their acts should not be illegal, or from the jury's wish to avoid the disagreeable job of convicting them.

The Prosecution's Strategy

In trying to prove the defendants guilty beyond a reasonable doubt, the prosecutors will present evidence to establish:

- the *motive* for the robbery and murders;
- *premeditation* (the design or plan to kill);
- the *opportunity* to commit the crime (that they were present at the scene of the crime);
- the *means* (weapon) and *capacity* (physical strength) to commit the crime;
- that their actions after the crime (lying, concealing information) showed their guilt.

The Defense's Strategy

In trying to prove the defendants not guilty beyond a reasonable doubt, the defense lawyers will cross-examine the prosecution's witnesses, hoping to cast doubt on their testimony. The defense will challenge whether the witness's story is accurate or believable. Sometimes the defense will try to show that the witness told a different story about the same thing at another time. The defense will also suggest other explanations for damaging testimony. These explanations will be more fully developed when the defense presents its case.

Prosecution Witnesses

Monday, June 6, 1921, afternoon

Three medical experts presented the results of the autopsies. Berardelli died shortly after he was shot. Four bullets were found in his body. The fatal bullet went in at the back of his shoulder, pierced his right lung, moved downward, and ended up in his hipbone. Parmenter died the day after the robbery. Five bullets went through his body.

Wednesday, June 8, 1921
Witness: Shelly A. Neal

Neal picked up the payroll at the railroad station. When he delivered it, he saw the getaway car parked in front of the Slater & Morrill upper factory. He described the car as a seven-passenger Buick with a canvas top. The top was closed. There were side curtains and a little back curtain coming up to the first rib of the top. Neal could not see into the car.

Neal described one of the robbers as slight and slim, with extremely light hair, blue eyes, and a very pale complexion.

Thursday, June 9, 1921
Witness: James Bostock
Direct Examination by the Prosecution

Bostock was about 60 feet from the shooting, but could not identify the shooters.

Q. Please tell us what you saw on April 15.
A. I was walking past the excavation when Parmenter called out to me. I said a few words to him, then turned to leave and heard shots. I swung

Excavation site is on left, in between water tank and house

around. Berardelli was on his knees, and this man about five feet away from him was shooting. Parmenter got about thirty feet across the street when he was hit.

I started toward Berardelli. I was about 50 or 60 feet away from him when one bandit swung around and shot at me twice. I headed for the railroad crossing. The man near Berardelli signaled down the road, and a black Buick came up the street. A third man appeared from somewhere, I don't know where. He helped throw the payroll boxes into the car. They all jumped into the car, and it drove away.

Q. Please describe the bandits.

A. They were dressed in darkish clothes, with dark caps. They were medium build, smoothed faced and dark complected. They appeared to be foreigners. I thought they was Italian fruit peddlers.

The prosecutor hoped to prove that the gun found on Vanzetti when he was arrested was Berardelli's gun. He believed Sacco had taken it from Berardelli and given it to Vanzetti later on.

Q. Do you know if Berardelli had a revolver?

A. Yes, I seen him a number of times with it. I joked with him about it, I asked him if he carried it to shoot rats. It was a .38 caliber, but I don't know what kind.

Cross-Examination by the Defense

The defense wanted to disprove that Berardelli had his gun that day.

Q. When you saw Berardelli that morning, did you see his gun?
A. No. He said he had it in his pocket, but he didn't take it out.

The defense showed Bostock the gun found on Vanzetti.

Q. Is this Berardelli's gun?
A. I don't know.

Be the Jury

Did Berardelli have his gun that day?

Witness: **Lewis L. Wade**
Direct Examination by the Prosecution

Wade was about 150 feet away from the shooting. His description of the shooting matched Bostock's. He did not positively identify Sacco.

Q. Please describe the man who shot Berardelli.
A. He was about twenty-five or twenty-seven. Kind of short, with short-cropped black hair. He needed a shave. He weighed about 140 pounds.

Wade's description of the robber resembled that of Sacco, who was twenty-nine at the time of the robbery.

Q. Have you seen that man since that day?
A. I thought I saw him at the Brockton police station about a month after the shooting. But a few weeks ago I was in a barber shop and a man came in who looked just like the man who shot Berardelli. So I would not say for sure now. But Sacco looks somewhat like the robber.

Cross-Examination by the Defense

The defense needed to downplay Wade's partial identification of Sacco. Wade's testimony from the preliminary hearing was submitted. Written records of hearings are often used at trials to point out differences in witness testimony. Once the judge accepts testimony, it can be referred to during the trial, and it can be read into the trial record. At the hearing Wade had said that he was unsure that Sacco was one of the shooters.

Q. At the hearing you said, "I have a little doubt about positively identifying Sacco." Then you were asked, "Will you say positively that this is the man?" And you answered, "No." Do you remember saying this?

A. I don't know, it's so long ago.

Q. Do you remember the next day telling three workers that you thought the bandits were around twenty?

A. No.

Be the Jury

Could Sacco resemble the robber, but not be the robber?

It was the hottest day of the year. Fans were brought into the room. By the afternoon, Judge Thayer told the jurors to take off their jackets.

Witness: **Mary E. Splaine**
Examination by the Prosecution

Splaine, a bookkeeper, saw the getaway car from the second-story window of the Slater & Morrill upper factory.

Q. What did you see from your window?
A. When the Buick was halfway across the railroad track, I saw a man in it. He was slightly taller than I am. He weighed about 145 pounds. He was muscular. He wore a gray shirt. His face was clean cut. His forehead was high. His hair was brushed back, and it was about two and a half inches long. He had dark eyebrows. His complexion was a peculiar white that looked greenish. I noticed particularly that his left hand was a good-sized hand, a hand that showed strength. It was placed on the back of the front seat.
Q. How long was he in your view?
A. About four seconds.

Splaine positively identified Sacco as the man.

Cross-Examination by the Defense

Q. Was this man leaning against the front seat shooting a gun?
A. I didn't see him fire anything.

The defense read Splaine's testimony from the hearing: She had said then that the man in the car was shooting a gun. Now she denied that she had said it. The defense pointed out more contradictions in her testimony to discredit her identification.

Q. What was the man in the car doing?
A. His left hand was on the back of the front seat. I never saw his right hand.
Q. But the transcript says you saw his right hand. Is it incorrect?
A. It's incorrect so far as my saying I saw his right hand. I never saw it. I never said so.

Splaine's voice was angry and defiant.

Q. Do you remember being asked, "Do you say this is the man?" and answering, "I will not swear positively he is the man. I did not get a sufficient look to say positively this is the man."
A. I would not answer that question that way.

The defense believed it was impossible for Splaine to have seen so many details in a few seconds from so far away.

Q. You gave a great many details about a man you had never seen before. Are these details based on what you saw in four seconds from a second-story window eighty feet away?

A. Yes.

Q. How many times did you go to the jail to see Sacco?

A. Three times.

Q. Did you ever see him in a lineup?

A. No.

Friday, June 10, 1921
Redirect Examination by the Prosecution

The prosecutor examined Splaine again to clear up any confusion in her testimony. The prosecution didn't want the jury to look unfavorably on Splaine because she had denied her testimony at the hearing. She admitted that at the hearing she had said that she had doubts about Sacco, but she insisted she had no doubts now. He positively was the man she had seen.

Be the Jury

Could anyone see so many details in four seconds?

Why did Splaine give different testimony at the hearing?

Witness: **Louis Pelser**
Direct Examination by the Prosecution

Pelser worked on the first floor of the Rice & Hutchins factory, right across from where the killings were. He was the second witness to place Sacco at the scene of the crime.

Q. What did you see on April 15?

A. I heard three shots. I opened the middle window at the end of the factory about four inches. I looked out for about a minute and seen this fellow about seven feet away shoot once at Berardelli. He wore a dark-green pair of pants and an army shirt. He had

very dark wavy hair pushed back. He was dark-skinned. His gun was bright and shiny. I wouldn't swear it was him, but Sacco is a dead image of that man.

Cross-Examination by the Defense

The defense set out to show how limited Pelser's view was.

Q. The factory windows are frosted, so they have to be opened to see anything. So you were looking out of a window open about four inches. And the window ledge sticks up about eight to twelve inches. So your vision was about eight to twelve inches?
A. Yes. Then I opened the window wide and looked out. Everything happened in about a minute.

The defense hoped to discredit Pelser by showing that he had lied to a defense investigator and the police.

Q. Mr. Reid, who works for me, talked with you about four months ago. Did you tell him everything you knew about this case?
A. Not everything. I told him some part of the story. I didn't tell him the whole story because I didn't want to be a witness in court.
Q. Did you also lie to the police?
A. Yes, for the same reason. I didn't want to be a witness.

Q. You told Mr. Reid that while they were shooting, you ducked under a bench. But today you said that you looked out that open window. Which is the truth?

A. I ducked under the table.

Be the Jury

How clearly could Pelser see from his window?

If Pelser ducked, did he have enough time to see Sacco?

If Pelser lied before, is he telling the truth now?

Saturday, June 11, 1921
Witness: Lola R. Andrews
Direct Examination by the Prosecution

Andrews, the prosecution's star witness, wore a stiff-crowned hat with a flat brim that hid much of her face. She claimed to have talked with Sacco.

Q. Tell us about April 15.
A. I was near the Slater & Morrill upper factory when I saw a light-complected man leaning on a car. A dark man was working under the car. He got up from under the car. I asked him if he would please show me how to get into the factory. I wanted to see about a job. He spoke clearly and asked me which factory I wanted. I said Rice & Hutchins. He told me where to go.

When Andrews identified Sacco as the man, he stood up in the cage and called out in heavily accented English, "Do you mean me? Take a good look." She did not respond. A court officer told Sacco to sit down, and he did.

The courtroom buzzed after Sacco's outburst. Except to answer "present" at the opening of each session, he had been silent during the trial. Sometimes he whispered to Vanzetti or his lawyer. During recess he usually talked with his wife and played with the baby.

The judge called the court to order, and the defense began its cross-examination.

Cross-Examination by the Defense

Andrews was grilled about her identification of Sacco.

Q. Where did you identify Sacco?

A. I went in February to the Dedham jail. I went into a room with a grating in the back. For about ten minutes I looked through the grating down into this other room. I saw a man pacing back and forth.

Q. Was he all alone?

A. I don't know. I can't remember. Maybe he was. Maybe there were others.

Q. What was he wearing?

A. I don't know.

Q. Do you mean that you can't remember his clothing in February, five months ago, but you can remember it from the robbery, a year and a half ago?

A. I wasn't there to look at his clothing. I came to look at his face.

After three hours of questioning, Andrews fainted and was carried out of the courtroom on the chair she was seated on. The judge called a recess until she felt better.

Monday, June 13, 1921

The defense's cross-examination of Andrews continued. Andrews was questioned at length about photographs of men, including Sacco, that had been shown to her by the defense in January. She denied ever seeing the pictures. A written record of the talk showed that she had seen the pictures and had not identified Sacco's then. The defense asked Andrews if he had tried to influence her when he had shown her the photographs. Andrews said that he had offered her a trip to Maine. The idea that the defense might have bribed a witness could destroy its believability with the jury. The matter needed to be cleared up.

Q. Do you mean that I offered you a vacation?

A. Well, you asked me for the address in Maine of my friend Mrs. Julia Campbell. Then you asked if I had ever visited her there. I said, "No." You asked me if I would like to go there. I told you I couldn't go at that time. You said, "How would you like a little vacation?" I told you I couldn't because I might lose my job. And you said, if I lost my job, you would see I got a job as good as I had now, or better.

Q. Did I offer you anything to testify in any particular way?

A. Well, I don't know how to answer that. The only

thing I can say is you were giving me this chance to go to Maine.

Q. Do you remember after leaving the Dedham jail telling a man named Harry Kurlansky, "I am tired of this thing. They wanted me to say that I have seen the robber. But I said, 'How can I? I can't recognize him'?"

A. I don't remember seeing or talking to Harry that day.

Be the Jury

How could Sacco be the man who spoke so clearly to Andrews when he speaks English with such a thick accent?

Why couldn't Andrews remember if she saw Sacco in a lineup or alone?

How could Andrews identify Sacco in February at the jail if she didn't identify him in the photograph in January?

Was the defense trying to bribe Andrews? If she thought so, why didn't she report it to the prosecutor?

Witness: **Michael Levangie**
Direct Examination by the Prosecution

Michael Levangie was gate tender at the railroad crossing diagonally across from the Slater & Morrill upper factory. He was the only witness who said Vanzetti drove the getaway car.

Q. What did you see at the crossing?
A. I heard gunshots just when the bell signaled an approaching train. A car was coming up the hill, going about eighteen miles an hour. It came to the gates, which were down. Then there was a revolver pointed at my head from the left-hand side of the car. The car was about twelve feet from me. I looked back to see if there was time to let the car go through before the train came. There was, so I let it go. The driver was Vanzetti.

Cross-Examination by the Defense

The defense pointed out contradictory statements made by Levangie two weeks earlier, hoping to cast doubt on his testimony.

Q. Do you remember two weeks ago telling me that the only view you had of the man was through the windshield, and that you couldn't see the driver because of the curtains?

A. I don't remember.

Q. Are you saying I never spoke to you two weeks ago?

A. I don't remember anything about it.

Be the Jury

Why did Levangie tell a different story to the defense lawyer?

Which story is true?

Witness: **John W. Faulkner**
Direct Examination by the Prosecution

Faulkner said that Vanzetti was on an early morning train for Boston on April 15. The prosecution believed his testimony showed that the robbery had been premeditated: One part of the plan was to pick Vanzetti up at East Braintree and take him to South Braintree.

Q. What did Vanzetti say to you on the train?
A. Three times before we got to East Braintree, he asked if we were there. I told him I would let him know when we got there. He got off at East Braintree carrying a leather bag.

Cross-Examination by the Defense

The defense tried to show how unobservant Faulkner was.

Q. You rode that train every day. Did you see anybody you knew?
A. Not that I remember.
Q. Who was the conductor on the train?
A. I don't know.
Q. Who was the brakeman?
A. I don't know.

The defense asked an unidentified man in the courtroom to stand up.

Q. Is that the man who sat next to you?
A. I never saw that gentleman to my knowledge.

Be the Jury

If Faulkner doesn't remember other people on the train, how good is his memory?

What did the voice of the man on the train sound like?

Tuesday, June 14, 1921
Witness: Harry Dolbeare
Direct Examination by the Prosecution

Dolbeare was originally called as a juror. When he saw Vanzetti in the courtroom, he remembered seeing him on that April 15. He told the prosecutor and became a witness.

Q. Please tell us what you saw on April 15.
A. Sometime between 10 A.M. and noon, I saw a large, rather dusty car come up Holbrook Avenue in South Braintree and turn into Washington Street. Five men were in it, two on the front seat. One man looked like a foreigner. He had a very heavy mustache, quite dark. He attracted my attention because he was leaning forward from the backseat as though he was either talking to the driver or the other person in the front of the car.

Then Dolbeare identified Vanzetti as the man with the mustache.

Cross-Examination by the Defense

The defense believed that prejudice against immigrants had distorted Dolbeare's identification.

Q. What attracted your attention to the men?

A. Their appearance. They looked strange to me, like strangers in town, like a carload of foreigners. I felt they were a tough-looking bunch.

Q. Can you remember anything of their faces or clothes?

A. No.

Q. Were their faces smooth faced, clean, dirty, grimy?

A. I couldn't say.

Q. Is there any other way that you would characterize these men except as a tough-looking bunch?

A. No.

Be the Jury

Does Dolbeare think all foreigners look alike?

Wednesday, June 15, 1921
Witness: Austin Reed
Direct Examination by the Prosecution

Reed was the gate tender at the railroad crossing in Matfield. About 4:15 P.M. the getaway car reached the crossing.

Q. What happened at the crossing?
A. I saw a dark-colored car coming at the same time as a train. I went outside with my sign to tell the car to stop. It stopped about 40 feet from me, but the motor was still running. The man sitting next to the driver asked, what to hell was I holding him up for? He pointed his finger at me. The men in the car were talking among themselves and seemed quite anxious to go by. The car drove away and then returned after a few minutes, and recrossed the tracks. After the train went by, the car crossed the tracks again. The same man pointed his finger at me again and says, "What to hell did you hold us up for?" Then the car speeded away. That man was Vanzetti.

Cross-Examination by the Defense

The defense sought to show that Reed was also prejudiced against foreigners and it had distorted his identification of Sacco and Vanzetti.

Q. When you saw newspaper photographs of the defendants what nationality did you think they were?
A. Italian.
Q. So when you went to the police station, you expected to see Italians, didn't you?

Reed hesitated. The defense asked the question again.

A. Yes, I expected to see Italians.
Q. When the man in the car called out, "What in hell did you stop us for?" he was 40 feet away and the car motor was running and a train was coming. Could you hear his voice loud and strong with all this noise?
A. Yes. I heard him speak in clear English.

Be the Jury

Was Reed's identification influenced by his belief that the men were Italian?

Levangie testified that Vanzetti was the driver. Reed said Vanzetti sat next to the driver. Who is right?

What does Vanzetti's voice sound like?

How many people have placed the defendants near or at the scene of the crime?

How reliable are these identifications?

Friday, June 17, 1921
Witness: **Michael Connolly**
Direct Examination by the Prosecution

The prosecution believed that the defendants' lies, along with their interactions with police officer Connolly, revealed their guilt. Under the law anything said at the time of arrest can be used against the accused. Untruths told upon arrest are evidence of consciousness of guilt.

Q. Tell us about the arrest.
A. The police dispatcher had told me to pick up two foreigners on the Brockton streetcar. I got on and looked around for two foreigners. When I saw them, I asked them where they came from. They said, "Bridgewater." I said, "What was you doing in there?" They said, "We went to see a friend of mine." I said, "Who?" He said, "A man they call Pappi." "Well," I said, "you are under arrest." Vanzetti was sitting toward the window. He put his hand in his hip pocket, and I says, "Keep your hands out on your lap, or you will be sorry."

Vanzetti called out, "You are a liar!"
Connolly continued:

They asked what they were arrested for. I says, "Suspicious characters." About three minutes later Officer Vaughn got on the streetcar. He frisked

'LIAR!' SHOUTS
VANZETTI TO
POLICE WITNESS

Headline from *The Boston Herald*

Vanzetti and found a loaded gun in his left hip back pocket. I gave Sacco a slight going over.

In the police car I told them that on the first false move, I would put a bullet in them. Sacco reached his hand under his overcoat. I says, "Have you got a gun there?" He says, "I ain't got no gun." "Well," I says, "keep your hands outside of your clothes." We went along a little further and he done the same thing. I gets up on my knees on the front seat, and I reaches over and puts my hands under his coat, but I did not see any gun. "Now," I says, "Mister, if you put your hand in there again, you are going to get into trouble." He says, "I don't want no trouble." When we reached the station, I searched Vanzetti. I found twenty dollars and four bullets in his coat pocket. Officer Spear found some bullets in Sacco's hip pocket and a loaded .32 Colt.

Saturday, June 18, 1921
Cross-Examination by the Defense

The defense wanted to show that many people had gone to identify the defendants at jail. Most of them could not positively identify them. Only the ones who could had testified. However, police officer Connolly could not remember how many people may have been shown the prisoners.

Q. About how many people came to identify the defendants?

A. I haven't the slightest idea.

Q. Was it fifteen, twenty-five, or fifty, or eighty, or anywhere in there?

A. I couldn't say.

Q. But every time people were brought in to see the prisoners, you were there?

A. Yes.

Be the Jury

Why were Sacco and Vanzetti carrying loaded guns?

How many people came to see the defendants and could not identify them?

Monday, June 20, 1921
Witness: George Kelley
Direct Examination by the Prosecution

Kelley was the superintendent of the factory where Sacco worked. He was also Sacco's friend. The prosecution pressed Kelly to say that the cap found on the street near Berardelli's body was Sacco's.

Q. What kind of cap did Sacco wear to work?

A. A dark cap. I never looked much at it to notice any details. Sacco hung it up on a nail.

The prosecutor showed Kelley a cap with a tear in the inside lining. The prosecutor believed the lining had gotten torn from being hung up on a nail in the factory.

Q. Does this cap look like Sacco's cap?

A. The only thing I could say about that cap, from seeing it on a nail in the distance, is that it is similar in color. As far as details, I could not say it was the same cap.

Q. Did anything happen to the lining in Sacco's cap because it was hung up on a nail?

A. I don't know.

The prosecutor asked to put the cap in evidence. The defense objected that there was no evidence to link the cap with Sacco except that it looked somewhat like his cap. The defense felt if the cap was admitted in evidence, it would be highly prejudicial to Sacco—it would make jurors think his cap had been found at the scene of the crime. The defense exercised its right to object to having the cap admitted as evidence. When a judge *sustains* (upholds) the objection, the evidence is not admitted. If the judge *overrules* the objection, the evidence is admitted.

Judge Thayer accepted the cap as evidence.

Cross-Examination by the Defense

Q. You had about 185 employees last April. How many workers wore caps?
A. I don't know.
Q. Do you remember what cap Sacco wore last April to the factory?
A. No, sir.

Be the Jury

Can anyone positively identify that cap as Sacco's?

Witness: **Lincoln Wadsworth**

The prosecution wanted to prove that the gun found on Vanzetti had been taken from Berardelli, because that would conclusively prove that he was one of the robbers. Before the murder, Berardelli had taken his gun to be repaired. Wadsworth, a clerk at the repair shop, testified that he had received the gun and that it was the same caliber and make as the gun found on Vanzetti.

But no one at the repair shop had marked down the serial number of Berardelli's gun, so it could not be conclusively proved that Vanzetti's gun was Berardelli's. And the gun was no longer at the shop.

Witness: **George Fitzemeyer**

Fitzemeyer, a repairman at Iver Johnson, contradicted Wadsworth. He testified that Berardelli's revolver was a .32, not a .38. He also said Berardelli's gun had needed a new hammer, not a spring. He had examined Vanzetti's revolver and testified that it had a new hammer.

Be the Jury

If Berardelli's gun is not at the shop, where is it?

Tuesday, June 21, 1921
Witness: William H. Proctor
Direct Examination by the Prosecution

Proctor had been a police captain for sixteen years. He was one of four ballistics experts (two for the prosecution, two for the defense) who had fired bullets from Sacco's gun into oiled sawdust. They had compared these shells with the four bullets taken from Berardelli's body and with four spent shells found at the scene of the crime. All experts agreed that three of the spent shells could not have been fired from Sacco's gun. One, bullet No. 3, could have been. In 1921 ballistics experts were not as sophisticated as they are today.

Q. Please explain how you decide what make and type of gun a bullet has been fired from?
A. We measure the width of the grooves on the bullets caused by the lands in the pistol. The lands are raised-up places in the pistol that have grooves between them. When the bullet is fired, the lands make a groove or marks on it. The lands reverse where the grove is in the pistol. When a bullet is fired, it's given a twist coming out of the gun barrel. To identify a bullet, we measure the marks and compare them with other bullets fired from the same gun.

Q. Tell me your opinion as to what type of weapon bullet No. 3 was fired from.

A. Bullet No. 3 is a Winchester make, W.R.A. It was fired by a Colt automatic revolver, .32 caliber.

Q. What is your basis for that opinion?

A. This bullet has a left-hand twist instead of a right. Also, the grooves made by the pistol while passing through on this bullet are .060 of an inch and I don't know of any other pistol than a Colt automatic that gives a groove like that.

Q. Do you know of any other automatic pistol that gives a left-hand twist to the bullet?

A. All give a right-hand twist, but none other give a left-hand twist.

Q. Have you an opinion as to whether bullet No. 3 was fired from Mr. Sacco's Colt?

A. Yes. My opinion is that it is consistent with being fired by that pistol.

Cross-Examination by the Defense

To diminish the impact of Proctor's testimony, the defense tried to show that he was not an expert about Colt revolvers.

Q. Do you have any opinion as to how much that gun has been used?

A. No.

Q. Do you know what the maximum pressure pounds per square inch is on a Colt automatic .32?

A. I don't know anything along that line. My experience is in examining, measuring, and comparing bullets.

Witness: **Charles Van Amburgh**
Direct Examination by the Prosecution

Van Amburgh, the second gun expert, agreed with Proctor that bullet No. 3 had come from Sacco's gun.

Q. After your tests, have you any opinion as to whether or not the No. 3 bullet was fired from Mr. Sacco's gun?

A. I am inclined to believe that it was fired from his gun.

Q. Why?

A. I measured the marks on that bullet and compared them with the width of the impressions taken of Sacco's gun barrel. I also measured the width of marks in the bullets that we shot into the oiled sawdust. There were irregularities in the bullets we shot through Sacco's gun. They were caused by pitting (rust) in the barrel. The pitting on the inside of the barrel is one inch in from the muzzle at the right-hand side of the lands. This pitting causes streaks along the edge of the groove in the bullets. There is one very pronounced streak along the edge of the No. 3 bullet.

Headline from *The Boston Herald*

Van Amburgh agreed with Fitzemeyer that Vanzetti's gun had a new hammer.

Cross-Examination by the Defense

The defense called attention to the fact that many older Colts have pitting (rust) marks.

Q. Is it rare in a two-year-old revolver to have rust or little cavities in the barrel?
A. I would not say it was rare. I would say it is quite common.
Q. So we could find this condition in other Colts?
A. I believe that is right.
Q. Are you absolutely sure these marks were caused by rust?
A. No.

The prosecution ended its case.

Be the Jury

Is the evidence strong enough to show that bullet No. 3 came from Sacco's gun?

Has it been proved that Vanzetti's gun was Berardelli's?

The Defense's Opening Statement

Wednesday, June 22, 1921

The defense began its case with an opening statement by William Callahan, the lawyer who had originally represented Sacco and Vanzetti:

We start the defendants' case at the same place the government opened its case; that is, we presume under law that the defendants are innocent. The burden of proof is still upon the government. The defendants do not have to testify, but they will. They will clear up many points brought up by the prosecution, including why they were armed the night they were arrested.

The defense will be made up of two parts: witnesses who were at or near the scene of the shooting will tell you what and whom they saw. The defendants will explain what they were doing on April 15.

On the day of the robbery Sacco was at the Italian consulate in Boston getting his passport so he and his family could go to Italy to visit his sick father. A consulate official will confirm that he saw Sacco. Other people will testify that Sacco was in Boni's restaurant in Boston later that day. Witnesses will confirm that Vanzetti was in Plymouth that day. Their evidence will convince you that the defendants could not have been in South Braintree on April 15.

Frank Burke and Albert Frantello will tell you what they saw. Winfred Pierce, who worked at the window directly above Miss Splaine's, will describe what he saw. You will learn that several government witnesses said different things before the trial from what they said at the trial. This will make you change your mind about the reliability of their testimony at this trial.

I ask you to give the defendants and their witnesses the same consideration, attention, and patience that you gave the government witnesses.

The Defense's Strategy

In trying to prove Sacco and Vanzetti not guilty beyond a reasonable doubt, the defense will present witnesses to:

- cast further doubt on damaging testimony given by prosecution witnesses;
- establish alibis for each defendant;

The defense will also offer other theories and evidence to:

- explain the defendants' actions after the murders (lying to the police, concealing information, carrying weapons).

The Prosecution's Strategy

The prosecutor will cross-examine the defense's witnesses and try to cast doubt on their believability and their accounts of events.

Defense Witnesses

Witness: Frank Burke
Direct Examination by the Defense

Burke had arrived in South Braintree around 2:30 P.M. to give a glass-blowing exhibition. He was the first witness to testify that neither defendant was in the getaway car.

Q. What did you see near the railroad crossing?
A. I seen a Buick coming about eight miles an hour toward the track. Two men jumped on the running board and got into the backseat. Then one man in the back climbed into the front and sat next to the driver. A shot was fired from the car. A man ran up the street hollering, "Stop them! Stop them!" The man on the front seat leaned slightly forward, grabbed hold of the door, snapped a gun at me, and said, "Get out of the way, you son of a B."
Q. Did you see the man?
A. Yes, sir. He was within ten feet of me.
Q. Was either defendant this man?
A. No, sir.

Burke's description of the man differed from everyone else's.

SAYS SACCO AND VANZETTI NOT IN BANDITS' CAR

Witness Burke Tells of Seeing Slayers of Paymaster in Flight

Headline from *The Boston Herald*

Cross-Examination by the Prosecution

The prosecutor focused on how long Burke saw the men.

Q. How long did you watch the man climbing to the front?
A. I guess it was less than a minute.
Q. How much less than a minute?
A. I don't know.

Be the Jury

Did Burke get a closer view than most prosecution witnesses?

Thursday, June 23, 1921
Witness: Alberto Frantello
Direct Examination by the Defense

Frantello said that at 3 P.M., he saw two men about ten feet away leaning against a railing outside the Rice & Hutchins factory.

One was about thirty years old: He was stocky and dark haired, and weighed about 145 pounds. The other man, who was about twenty years old, was fair and had light hair. The dark-complexioned man was criticizing the other man. Frantello said he had stopped and looked at their faces for a second.

Q. What language were they using?

A. They were speaking in the American language.

Q. How near were you to them when they were talking?

A. I could have touched them.

Frantello stated forcefully that Sacco and Vanzetti were not these two men.

Cross-Examination by the Prosecution

The prosecutor set out to prove that Frantello was a poor eyewitness.

Q. Please step down from the witness stand. Then stop opposite two jurymen and look at them for about one second. Then describe them.

Frantello did as requested. When the prosecutor questioned him about the two jurors, he described one man as having a mustache and wearing a watch chain. Both men were clean shaven. Neither had a watch chain.

Q. Didn't you really only see these two men for about one second?

A. It was long enough so that it is in my mind yet.

Be the Jury

Did Frantello have less time to see the robbers than other witnesses who were farther away?

Defense Eyewitnesses

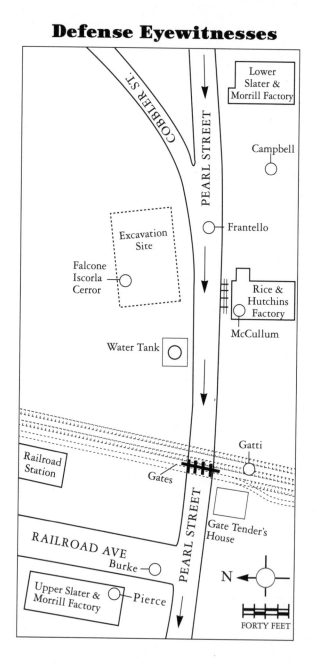

Witnesses: **Emilio Falcone, Pedro Iscorla, and Henry Cerror**

All three men worked at the excavation site about 50 feet away from the shooting. They all testified that neither defendant resembled the shooters. But each man described the shooters slightly differently. All three men spoke Spanish and used interpreters.

The heat in the courtroom was stifling. In the afternoon the temperature reached 94 degrees Fahrenheit.

Witness: **Winfred Pierce**

Pierce, a shoe cutter, said he had looked out a third-story window in the Slater & Morrill upper factory and seen the getaway car moving about twelve miles an hour over the railroad crossing. It was about 80 feet away. His description of the man climbing from the backseat to the front differed from Splaine's, though his view was similar. He insisted that neither defendant was the man.

Friday, June 24, 1921
Witness: Peter McCullum
Direct Examination by the Defense

Shoe cutter McCullum worked directly in front of the window, at the other end of the room from Pelser. The defense believed his testimony discredited Pelser's identification of Sacco.

Q. What did you see?

A. I lifted the window up and saw a man with a shiny gun in his left hand putting something into the backseat of the getaway car. As soon as the shooting started, I closed the window and laid down under a bench for a minute or two. Pelser got under his bench, too. We all stayed there for about two minutes. Then I got up and opened the first window on the west side of the factory. I saw Pelser standing at the first window at the east corner. He was hollering, "Get the number of the license plate." But I didn't see him do anything. About fifteen minutes later, I heard him say, "I didn't see any of the men, but I got the number of the car."

McCullum testified that neither defendant was the man with the shiny gun.

Cross-Examination by the Prosecution

Q. When you were under the bench where was Pelser?

A. Under his bench.

Q. Did Mr. Pelser tell you he didn't see anybody?

A. He did not tell me directly. We were all talking together about what was going on. He told all of us.

No one had seen the robber take anything from Berardelli, but the prosecutor suggested that the shiny gun in the left hand of one robber was the one found on Vanzetti.

Q. Did you get any view of that shiny gun?

A. Yes, it looked white.

The prosecutor laid Sacco's black gun and Vanzetti's nickel-plated gun on the table.

Q. Which gun looks like the one in the robber's hand?

A. That one.

McCullum pointed to Vanzetti's gun.

Be the Jury

Why did Pelser tell the other workers he hadn't seen the robbers if he had?

Does McCullum's testimony prove that Vanzetti's gun was Berardelli's?

Saturday, June 25, 1921
Witness: Nicola Gatti
Direct Examination by the Defense

Gatti, a railroad worker, testified through an interpreter that he heard shots when he was cleaning the ties on the tracks. He ran toward the factory and saw a car with five men. The defense considered Gatti's account crucial, because he was the only eyewitness who knew Sacco.

Q. How near were you to the car?
A. Four or five feet.
Q. How long have you known Sacco?
A. I have known him between 1913 and 1918, when he was living at Milford. But I haven't seen him since then.
Q. Did you see either defendant in the car?
A. No, sir.

Cross-Examination by the Prosecution

The prosecutor emphasized Gatti's limited view to suggest that Sacco could have been in the car.

Q. Were there any curtains on the side of the car near you?

A. There were no curtains on the front part. There were curtains toward the back.

Q. How quickly did the car pick up speed after the gates were raised?

A. Well, I can't say as to the miles per hour, but it was going fast, very fast.

Q. Did you read any numbers on the rear of the car?

A. No, sir.

Be the Jury

Since Gatti knew Sacco, wouldn't he have recognized him if he was in the car?

Whose eyewitnesses had a clearer view of the robbers, the prosecution's or the defense's?

Have the defense eyewitnesses provided reasonable doubt that the defendants are not the robbers?

Monday, June 27 , 1921
Witness: Edward Brooks
Direct Examination by the Defense

Brooks was the ticket agent at the East Braintree railroad station. His testimony suggested that a man resembling Vanzetti got off at East Braintree.

Q. Did you see a man get off at East Braintree within a month or two after this shooting?

A. I did. He was a tall, thin man, carrying a bag. He wore a kind of brown, faded-out black suit. He had old dusty shoes on. I thought he was a workman. I see him six times within the last six months or a year. But I don't remember if I saw him the day of the murder.

Cross-Examination by the Prosecution

Q. Would you describe Mr. Vanzetti as a tall lanky man?

A. No, sir, not as tall as that man.

Q. When did you first see this man?

A. That's impossible to say. I know I've seen him get off several times.

Be the Jury

Could Faulkner have mistaken Vanzetti for this man?

Witnesses: **Henry McNaught, Ernest Pratt, and Harry Cash**

If Vanzetti had boarded the train to East Braintree, as the prosecution witness John Faulkner had claimed, Vanzetti would have bought a ticket. But conductor McNaught testified that no cash fares were bought from Plymouth to Seaside or to East or South Braintree on April 15.

Ticket agent Pratt said no cash fares were bought at Plymouth to East or South Braintree. Ticket agent Cash said that no cash fares were sold from Seaside to the Braintrees.

But on cross-examination the men testified that they did not know if any or how many tickets had been bought the day before.

Witness: **Julia Campbell**
Direct Examination by the Defense

Sixty-eight-year-old Julia Campbell, who was with Lola Andrews on April 15, contradicted Andrews' testimony.

Q. What did you see outside the Slater & Morrill factory?

A. I saw a car. A man in khaki clothes was standing about 5 feet away from the building. Another man was down underneath the car. He never looked up at all.

Q. Did you or Mrs. Andrews speak to the man down under the car?

A. No.

Q. Who did you talk to?

A. I didn't talk to anyone. Mrs. Andrews asked the man in the khaki clothes where the building entrance was. He told us, and we went there.

Q. Were you near Mrs. Andrews the whole time?

A. Yes, sir.

Headline from *The Boston Herald*

Cross-Examination by the Prosecution

After a few questions, the prosecutor felt concerned that because Campbell was elderly, she might tire from standing up in the witness box. "Are you tired?" he asked. She patted him on his shoulder and said, "I'm fine. I want to get on with this." The spectators laughed. But after a few more questions, for no visible reason, she started to cry. The judge called a recess for five minutes. After the recess, the prosecutor tried to cast doubt on her testimony.

Q. Now, aren't you confusing the man under the car with the man standing 5 feet away from it?
A. No, I am not.
Q. Could you see the face of the man under the car?
A. No—his cap was drawn down and he never looked up. I saw his cheek.
Q. How do you know Mr. Sacco is not the man?
A. Well, I don't know that he is not the man, but he don't look like the man I saw there.

Be the Jury

Who is telling the truth, Campbell or Andrews?

Witness: **Harry Kurlansky**
Direct Examination by the Defense

Kurlansky, a storekeeper in Quincy, had known Andrews about eight years. He described a talk he had with her in February. The defense hoped his testimony further proved that Andrews was a liar.

Q. Tell us about your talk with Mrs. Andrews.
A. She came into my store about 6:30 P.M. in February. I said, "You look kind of tired." She says, "Yes. They are bothering the life out of me." I says, "What?" She says, "The government took me down and wants me to identify those men and I don't know a thing about them. I have never seen them and I can't recognize them." She says, "Unfortunately I was at the factory to get a job."

Cross-Examination by the Prosecution

The prosecution tried to prove that Kurlansky's memory was inexact and unreliable.

Q. When in February did you talk with Mrs. Andrews?

A. I could not remember the dates. I got a lot of other business to attend to than thinking about the dates. I am quite sure it was in February.

Q. Did you make a note of this conversation?

A. Absolutely not.

Redirect by the Defense

Q. What else did Mrs. Andrews say about her interview with the police?

A. She said they had gone over her past life since she was fifteen. She was afraid they were going to bring in some trouble she had had with a Mr. Landers. The story wouldn't have been good for her reputation.

Be the Jury

Did Andrews lie about seeing Sacco?

Witness: **James E. Burns**
Direct Examination by the Defense

For thirty years Burns had worked for the U.S. Cartridge Company as a ballistics engineer, making ammunition. The defense showed the jury a photograph of bullet No. 3 and

pointed out that the groove was narrower at the bottom of the bullet than at the top. Then he showed Burns six bullets fired from the Sacco gun.

Q. Do these bullets have the same irregularity shown on bullet No. 3?

A. Not in my opinion. Bullet No. 3 doesn't compare at all with these six bullets.

Q. From what gun might bullet No. 3 be fired?

A. From a Colt or a Bayard, or a Steyer, or a Savage, or a Walther. The bullet is so deformed I couldn't measure its diameter. So I'm in doubt as to which gun it was fired from. There also was not enough pitting (rust) in the Sacco pistol to identify bullets fired through it.

Burns was shown the gun found on Vanzetti. The defense wanted to prove that Fitzemeyer had been wrong that it had a new hammer. If the gun didn't have a new hammer, it couldn't be Berardelli's gun.

Q. Is there a new hammer in this gun?
A. In my opinion the hammer is not any newer than the rest of the gun.

Cross-Examination by the Prosecution

Q. You said that bullet No. 3 could have been fired by a Colt or a Bayard or other guns. So you are not saying that bullet No. 3 was not fired from a Colt?
A. No, sir.

Tuesday, June 28, 1921
Witness: J. Henry Fitzgerald
Direct Examination by the Defense

Fitzgerald, the second gun expert, supervised the testing of guns for the Colt Company. He had previously been in charge of the revolver department for the Iver Johnson Company for six years.

Q. Do you think bullet No. 3 was fired from Sacco's gun?

A. No. My opinion is that it was not fired from that pistol. The lands marks on the No. 3 bullet do not correspond to the six bullets we fired from Sacco's gun. Bullet No. 3 isn't pronounced in the same way as those other bullets. I found no condition in the barrel of Sacco's gun that would cause a bullet to jump the lands as shown in bullet No. 3.

Q. When shells are fired, there is a flow back of the metal of the primer. Is this common or uncommon to find in shells used in automatics?

A. Common.

Cross-Examination by the Prosecution

The prosecution aimed to prove that Vanzetti's gun could have had a new hammer.

Q. I know you examined the pistol found on Mr. Vanzetti. Did your examination show that a new hammer was put in that gun in 1920?
A. I can't say what was done to the pistol in 1920. I can only answer that I think the hammer shows the same amount of wear as the rest of the pistol.

The prosecution asked that Fitzgerald's answer be stricken from the record. The judge agreed. Then the prosecution asked Fitzgerald the same question five more times. He answered it the same way he had the first time.

Be the Jury

How do I decide which gun experts are right?

Wednesday, June 29, 1921
Witness: Joseph Rosen
Direct Examination by the Defense

Rosen, a cloth peddler, was the first of three people who backed up Vanzetti's alibi.

Q. Did you see Mr. Vanzetti on April 15, 1920?
A. Yes. I seen him in Plymouth about 9:30 A.M. selling fish from a pushcart. We talked about my business. Then he took me to a house two blocks away, where he showed a woman the cloth I was trying to sell him. I had sold that woman some other cloth two months before. Vanzetti spoke to her in Italian. I didn't understand what they were talking about. We agreed on a price. It was then twelve o'clock. I heard the factory whistles blowing. We talked for about five more minutes. I left and went to Whitman, where I stayed the night.

The defense brought a woman into court for the purpose of identification. Rosen said he had seen her before.

Cross-Examination by the Prosecution

The prosecution grilled Rosen for an hour, testing his memory of random dates.

Q. Do you keep notes of the places and times you visit these towns?

A. No, sir.

Q. Then what you said about April 15 is entirely a matter of recollection?

A. Yes, sir.

Q. Did you sell anybody else anything in Plymouth that day?

A. It's kind of too hard to remember.

Q. It is pretty hard to remember any day except April 15, isn't it?

A. Well, I remember that because my wife paid the poll tax that day. Also because when I went to Whitman after that, everybody was talking about the Braintree murders.

Witness: **Alfonsina Brini**

When Brini entered the courtroom, the jurors saw that she was the woman Rosen had identified. Sacco had been a boarder at her house for four years. He was a close friend of her husband's. She testified that Vanzetti and Rosen had come to her house at about 11:30 A.M. on April 15. Vanzetti had showed her and her daughter a piece of cloth with one or two small holes in it that he was thinking of buying from Rosen.

When cross-examined, Brini said she had never seen Rosen before April 15, which contradicted Rosen's testimony that he had sold her cloth two months before. Brini used an interpreter.

Thursday, June 30, 1921
Witness: Melvin Corl

Corl, a fisherman who had known Vanzetti for five years, said he saw Vanzetti on April 15 about 2 P.M. Corl was painting his boat. Vanzetti came by the shore and talked with him for about an hour and a half.

Corl said he remembered the date because he had been painting his boat around that time. He had intended to put the boat in the water on April 16, but he hadn't finished it then. He finished it on April 17, his wife's birthday. He also remembered towing a boat from Duxbury that same day.

Be the Jury

Brini might lie for her friend, but would Rosen and Corl?

Is their way of fixing the date accurate enough?

Friday, July 1, 1921

Witness: Giuseppe Andrower
Direct Examination by the Defense

Andrower, a clerk at the Italian consulate in Boston, said that he had seen Sacco on April 15. About forty people came to the consulate that day instead of the usual two hundred. Sacco had brought an oversized photograph for his passport picture. Andrower and his boss had laughed about the photograph because no one had ever brought such a large one. Andrower fixed the date because he remembered looking at the calendar when he and his boss were laughing about the photograph.

Cross-Examination by the Prosecution

To show that Andrower's memory was poor, the prosecutor quizzed him about the name of every person he had talked with on April 15, 17, 19, 24, and 29, and May 2, 3, and 4. Andrower could not remember any names. Nor could he describe anyone else in detail.

Be the Jury

Why does Andrower remember Sacco and not other people who came on other days?

Witness: **Rexford Slater**
Direct Examination by the Defense

The defense maintained that Vanzetti's gun had been bought from someone else. Slater identified the gun found on Vanzetti and its case

as having originally belonged to his father-in-law.

Q. Who did you sell this gun to?
A. I sold it for four dollars to a workman named Riccardo Orciani sometime late in the fall of 1919.

The jurors and spectators listened attentively when they heard Orciani's name. He had been with the defendants the night they were arrested.

Q. How do you identify this gun case?
A. On account of this brass knob here; also that leather tear on the back and this little strap.
Q. How do you identify the gun?
A. Well, the enamel was off from the end of the barrel. It was also off over the cylinder. I can't remember on what side though. I know it was gone or started off from one side.

Cross-Examination by the Prosecution

The prosecutor tried to show how insubstantial Slater's identification was.

Q. Do you know if this gun differs from any other gun of the same make that has been used as much, with respect to the loss of the enamel?
A. Why no, I don't know. I don't know how another gun might appear.
Q. Then you don't know for sure that is the gun, do you?
A. Well, it looks exactly like it.

Be the Jury

Is Slater's way of identifying the gun accurate?

Is Orciani going to testify that he sold Vanzetti this gun?

Witnesses: **John D. Williams, Albert Bosco, Felix Guadagni, and Antonio Dentamore**

Four men testified that they had seen Sacco in Boni's Restaurant in Boston that day. Williams, Bosco, and Dentamore had never met Sacco before that date. Guadagni knew him well. Williams fixed the date because it was a Thursday and he always made the rounds of factories in that part of town on Thursday. Bosco and Dentamore said they remembered the date because they had talked with Guadagni about a banquet being held that evening for the editor of the *Boston Transcript*. The cross-examination revealed that the banquet was held at noon on April 15, not at night.

Be the Jury

If Andrower and these four men saw Sacco on April 15, how could he have been at the shootout?

Would any of these men lie to save Sacco?

Tuesday, July 5, 1921
Witness: Bartolomeo Vanzetti
Direct Examination by the Defense

The courtroom, which had been quite empty the last ten days, was packed. Vanzetti's name was called. The metal door of the cage was opened. Vanzetti went to the witness stand, raised his right hand, and took the oath. Despite the blistering heat he looked cool and calm. He wore a dark suit, a white shirt, and a tie. There was a slight sag of skin under his chin. His hair had thinned since he had been in jail. He had aged considerably over the last eight months.

Though Vanzetti's understanding of English was good, he spoke with an accent and often sounded awkward. But the defense thought it best for him to testify in English so that he would seem less foreign, since so many of the defense's witnesses had been immigrants and unable to testify in English.

Vanzetti recounted his early life in Italy and his life since coming to the States thirteen years before. He said that he had gone to Mexico in 1917 to avoid the draft. He described his day on April 15, starting with peddling fish, meeting Rosen, seeing Brini and Corl.

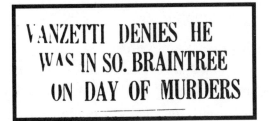

VANZETTI DENIES HE
WAS IN SO. BRAINTREE
ON DAY OF MURDERS

Headline from *The Boston Herald*

Then he explained that on April 22, his political friends had appointed him to go to New York City to learn about Salsedo. Salsedo had been picked up by the police during one of the raids on radicals. He had reportedly jumped from a prison window and killed himself.

The defense wanted the jury to understand

that the defendants had believed that Salsedo might have been pushed out of the window by the police. The defense strategy was to show that the defendants had lied when they were arrested because they feared they too might be deported or killed. Both men kept radical literature in their homes.

The prosecution objected to the testimony about Salsedo as being unrelated to the charges. The judge upheld the objection.

The defense wanted to show that Vanzetti's reason for carrying a gun had nothing to do with being a robber.

Q. Why did you get a gun?
A. Because it was a very bad time. There were many crimes, many holdups. And I like to have a revolver for self-defense. When I go to Boston for fish, I can carry eighty, one hundred, one hundred and twenty dollars.
Q. On May 5, you saw three bullets on Sacco's mantelpiece. Why did you take them?
A. I wanted to bring them to my friends in Plymouth who hunt. I put them in my pants back pocket. I don't remember if in my right or left side.

The defense claimed that the men needed Boda's car to move radical papers.

Q. Why did you need the car?

A. To go to Plymouth and ask friends to take about 400 pounds of literature from the houses of six people and put it in a proper place, where no policemen could get it. I was told in New York that it would be smart to do it. In that time the police were going through the house of many radicals and union organizers. They go there and take letters and books and newspapers, and put men in jail and deported many. Many have been misused in jail.

The defense switched the subject to Vanzetti's arrest. The jury was left with many unanswered questions about the recent raids on radicals.

Q. Please describe your arrest.

A. On the streetcar Officer Connolly asked, "Where do you come from?" and we answered, "We come from Bridgewater." Then he took out a revolver. He pointed it at me and say, "You don't move, you dirty thing."

Q. Did you put your hand in your clothes to take your gun out?

A. No.

Q. Did the police say to you, "Don't put your hand in there or I shoot?"

A. No.

The defense hoped the police's actions discredited them, built sympathy for Vanzetti, and showed why he had been so afraid to tell the truth.

Q. Did the police ever tell you why you were being arrested?

A. No, they never tell us. When I ask, they say, "Oh, you know why." And when I try to sleep in the cell, there is no blanket, only the wood. When we called for the blanket, they say, "Never mind, you catch warm by and by, and tomorrow morning we put you in a line in the hall between the chairs and shoot you."

The prosecutor called out, "Shoot?"

"Yes," said Vanzetti.

Judge Thayer asked, "Get shot?"

A. Yes. And one policeman, he spit three or four times at my face. Then he took a gun from his pocket. He pulled a bullet out of the gun, then put the bullet in the gun again and point the gun toward me. He maybe want to look to see if I get scared and go away from the cell door. I don't go away. I don't move.

Q. Why didn't you tell the police officer the truth?

A. I was afraid. Before I was arrested, I learned that my friend Salsedo jumped from the jail and killed himself. But we don't know if he really jumped. I thought they arrest me for political matters because of their questions. They asked me if I am a socialist, a communist, a radical.

Q. Did anyone tell you that you were suspected of robberies and murder?

A. No.

Be the Jury

Whom shall I believe, Connolly or Vanzetti?

Was Vanzetti so frightened because of his politics that he lied to the police?

How could Vanzetti be the man Reed heard speak English so clearly at Matfield Crossing?

Cross-Examination by the Prosecution

The prosecutor went right to how Vanzetti avoided the draft, hoping it would displease the jury, who would see it as unpatriotic.

Q. So you left Plymouth in 1917 when the country was at war so you would not have to fight as a soldier. Were you physically sound to be a soldier?
A. I don't refuse to go to war because of my physical condition or because I don't like this country or its people. I will refuse even if I was in Italy.

Takes Witness Stand in Own Defence —Tells Life Story—Admits Fleeing to Mexico to Escape Draft

Headline from *The Boston Herald*

The prosecutor didn't want the jury to believe the police had mistreated Vanzetti.

Q. You said a police officer pointed a loaded gun at you. What was that officer's name?
A. I do not know the name of any policeman of Brockton.
Q. Did you see that man among the officers here?
A. No.

The prosecutor wanted to disassociate himself from any mistreatment of Vanzetti.

Q. Did I treat you with discourtesy?

A. Oh, you treat me as a gentleman ought.

Q. You were willing to answer my questions?

A. I am not willing or unwilling. I do not know very well the language. I never was arrested before, but I have read that some people were kept in jail. So I don't refuse when the police take me to you or to the photographer, or to be recognized by the people. I don't refuse because I don't know that I have a right to refuse.

Q. Were you frightened?

A. I was not frightened that you punch me. I was disturbed.

The prosecutor read from the written record of Vanzetti's questioning on May 6 to show that he had told many lies that had had nothing to do with his radical politics. The questions came fast, and Vanzetti struggled with them in English.

Q. Is there any reason connected with the radical books that made you tell me that the gun cost you nineteen dollars when it cost you only five dollars?

A. No, there is no reason.

Q. Why did you lie about so many things?

A. Because I do not want to mention the names and houses of my friends.

Q. But you told us where your friend Pappi lived.

A. Yes, but he was my only friend who had no radical books in his house.

The prosecution wanted to undercut Vanzetti's claim that he had been worried about the books. The follow-up questions brought out that the two men hadn't moved that quickly to get rid of their radical papers.

Q. Did you think to get rid of Sacco's papers before May 5?

A. Yes, but we got no means to do it. We thought about putting them in the woods, but we do not want to spoil the books. We want to keep them.

Q. When you were first asked where you had been on April 15, you said you did not remember. Why after waiting months and months and months could you remember where you had been that day?

A. Not months and months and months, but three or four weeks after I see that I have to be careful and remember well if I want to save my life. I never dream that you will say that on April 15 that I went to steal and kill a man. April 15 is a day common to every other day to me. I peddled fish.

Be the Jury

If Vanzetti was so scared, why did he wait six days to try to get rid of the literature?

Why did Vanzetti lie about things not related to the radical books?

Thursday, July 7, 1921
Witness: Nicola Sacco
Direct Examination by the Defense

Sacco decided not to use an interpreter. He told about his life and work in Italy and the United States. He said he had "been crazy to come to America because he loved a free country." He explained that he had gone to Boston on April 15 to get a passport so he could go to Italy to see his sick father. He testified, as Vanzetti had, that he had lied because he thought he was being arrested for his radical politics and might be deported.

All through his testimony, Sacco stood with his hands folded. He answered each question quickly. Tension showed on his face as he struggled to express himself in English. His heavily accented English was hard to understand and many times the stenographer stopped him and asked him to repeat what he had said.

The defense showed Sacco the cap found near Berardelli's body. He denied ever having seen it before. When he tried it on, it perched on top of his head. Some spectators laughed. Sacco explained that his hat size was $7\frac{1}{8}$; this hat was $6\frac{7}{8}$.

Sacco's explanation of why he carried a gun was intended to show that he had no violent intentions.

Q. Why were you carrying a gun on May 5?

A. My wife cleaned the house because we are to go Saturday to New York to get the boat to Italy. She found the pistol then. I was afraid that sometime my boy could go after it. So I put the bullets and the gun in my pocket. I planned to go shooting in the woods with Vanzetti. But Vanzetti and I started to argue that afternoon, and I forget about shooting, so it was still in my pocket.

Be the Jury

If the cap doesn't fit Sacco, how can it be his?

Does the story about the gun make sense?

Friday, July 8, 1921
Cross-Examination by the Prosecution

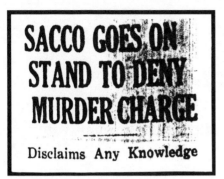

SACCO GOES ON STAND TO DENY MURDER CHARGE

Disclaims Any Knowledge

Headline from *The Boston Herald*

The prosecutor pressed Sacco about his avoiding the draft for World War I, hoping it would anger the jury.

Q. Yesterday you said you love a free country. Did you love this country in May 1917?
A. I don't want to say I did not love this country. I can't answer this in one word.

The prosecution asked the question four more times. Each time the defense objected that the question wasn't related to the charges. The judge overruled the defense and instructed Sacco to answer yes or no.

A. Yes, I loved this country.
Q. Did you go to Mexico to avoid being a soldier for this country that you loved?
A. Yes.
Q. Is that your way of showing your love for America?

Sacco hesitated.

A. Yes.

Q. And is your way of showing your love for your wife to run away from her?

A. I did not run away from her. I don't believe in war.

Q. Why didn't you stay down in Mexico?

Sacco hesitated. It was hard for him to find the right words in English to explain complicated ideas.

A. Well the first thing, I could not do my trade over there. And the food and the language was strange. And I was far away from my wife and boy. Over here is better industrial conditions and more chance for a working man.

Q. Is love of country among these reasons that you came back?

A. Yes sir, it's all together.

The defense objected to the whole line of questioning as unrelated to the charges and prejudicial against the defendants. The judge overruled the defense. Some reporters thought the judge was antagonistic to the defense.

Q. What did you mean when you said you loved a free country?

A. When I was a boy in Italy, I always thinking there is more chance here to raise the children, and get education. But when I came here, it was not what

I thought. I work hard here for twelve years but I could not put any money in the bank. Here I see the best and most intelligent men arrested, sent to prison, and died in prison. Eugene Debs,* a great man, is still in prison. Why? Because he is a socialist. He wanted the workers to have better conditions and better living, but they put him in prison.

Some of these rich men, like the Rockefellers and Morgans, they give a million dollars to colleges and people say they are great men. What good does these millions of dollars do for the working class? The poor man with a family of five can't live and send his children to Harvard if he wants to eat.

I love people who labor and work and who make no war. We don't want to destroy young men and fight by gun. War is for the great millionaires to make money. Why should I kill any man? What has he done to me?

Sacco's speech lasted ten minutes. His slender face grew tense trying to express his deep feelings in disconnected, broken English. The jurors and spectators listened intently to his every word.

Then the prosecutor recounted the lies Sacco had told him. These lies did not relate to Sacco's political beliefs and discredited his claim that he had lied because of those beliefs.

*Debs was a socialist and union organizer.

Q. You bought your gun in Milford but you told me you bought it in Boston. Why did you lie about such an innocent thing?

A. Because men could get one year jail for carrying a hidden weapon. It was just a mistake.

Q. You also lied about the bullets. You told me you didn't remember where you got them. You deliberately lied then, but now you say it was an innocent mistake.

A. Yes.

Q. If you told me the truth about where you bought the bullets, would that have led us to your friends who had radical papers?

A. No, sir.

The prosecution got Sacco to admit that he had also lied about how long he had known Vanzetti. Sacco said he lied about it because he hadn't wanted to tell about their evading the draft together in Mexico.

Q. About thirty people came to see if they could identify you. Did you think when Miss Splaine asked you to look this way and then that way, and then stoop over and hold a revolver, that they were looking you over because of your politics?

A. No, sir.

Q. Why did you think you were asked to get in those positions for?

A. I don't know.

The prosecution attacked Sacco's character by showing that he had also lied to his friend George Kelley.

Q. You told Mr. Kelley it was so crowded at the consulate that you missed the noon train. You lied to a man who trusted you. You live next door to him. He has been in your house many times and you have been in his house many times. And you told him a lie?

A. Yes.

Be the Jury

Why does the prosecution keep asking Sacco and Vanzetti about their politics if they are on trial for murder?

Could Sacco have been so scared of being deported that he lied about things that had nothing to do with his politics?

If Sacco is so trustworthy, why did he lie to his friend?

Sacco's cross-examination lasted six hours. Then Vanzetti's lawyers asked for a severance— a separate trial for Vanzetti. They were worried that Sacco's criticisms of America had made the jury dislike him. Sacco's testimony might so prejudice the jury that Vanzetti, who was being tried with him, would not get a fair verdict. The judge rejected the request.

Monday, July 11, 1921
Witness: James Matthews Hayes

Hayes and his wife had been spectators at the trial a week before. Sacco had recognized him as being on the train to Boston on April 15.

Sacco was taken out of the courtroom when Hayes testified that he had been on the train on April 15. Then Sacco was recalled as a witness. He described where he and Hayes had sat in the train car in relation to each other. Hayes was recalled as a witness. His recollection of where he had sat agreed exactly with Sacco's. The defense believed that by recognizing Hayes in court Sacco had proved he was on the train to Boston that day.

Be the Jury

If Sacco was on the train to Boston, then how could he have been in South Braintree?

The defense rested its case.

The Defense's Closing Statement

Tuesday, July 12, 1921

Now that both sides had presented their witnesses, the lawyers made closing statements. They summarized their viewpoints, contradicted and discredited the evidence from the other side, and appealed to the jury's emotions.

Listen carefully to the closing statement of Sacco's lawyer, Fred Moore. Separate the facts from his emotional presentation, for your verdict must be based on facts, not emotions.

There have been times during the last six weeks of this trial when I have felt that I, coming from 3,000 miles away in California, was an alien here in Massachusetts. If I, an American, have at times felt alien in thought and action, then how much more truly alien must these two defendants feel? They are sons of a foreign land. They have opinions and ideas foreign to most of us. But remember, render no verdict except upon the evidence, without fear or prejudice.

Many witnesses have testified for the prosecution. Neal said that the man he saw was neither defendant. Faulkner said he saw Vanzetti on the train to East Braintree. And yet Faulkner did not see a single man on that train whom he knew, even though he had ridden the train every day for years. He said there was a man sitting in the seat with him, but when I pointed out that man in court, Faulkner did not know him. But he says he recognizes Vanzetti, a man he had never seen before. His identification is wrong.

The government says Vanzetti got on the train to East Braintree. But none of the ticket agents at any of the stations along the route to Boston saw him. There is no record of a ticket bought on the train. Brooks said a month after the robbery he saw a man who looked like Vanzetti get off at East Braintree a few times. Is he lying? The government implied that the Buick picked up Vanzetti at East Braintree and drove him to South Braintree. But where is the evidence of this? You cannot take a man's life based on unproven testimony.

What about Mr. Bostock? He was within 60 feet of the bandits and he said he could not identify them. Now, our friend Wade, who was 150 feet away from the shooting, made a partial identification. The day after the robbery, Wade told three workers that he thought the robbers were nineteen or twenty years of age. When I questioned him about this, he said he didn't remember that. If you saw a man thirty years old committing a crime, would you say the next day that he was nineteen? No.

With bullets flying in all directions, and two men writhing on the ground in their death agonies, is it possible to identify someone as Wade claims, someone you have never seen before?

Levangie looked me in the eye and denied he had told me two weeks before that Vanzetti was the driver. He said he didn't know me because his conscience wasn't strong enough to stand the strain of talking to me after he had said those lies.

Miss Mary Splaine had never seen Sacco before. She saw him at best for only a few fleeting seconds. Yet remember all the details in her description of a man in a moving car on a floor below at least 60 feet away. Is her testimony believable? Or did she go to the police station three times to get all these details? Because she could not see these details from the second-floor window. You know it. I know it. And remember how she admitted at the hearing that she had doubts whether Sacco was the shooter.

How can we trust any of these identifications when the defendants were never identified in a lineup? Miss Splaine and those thirty others who came to look at the defendants never saw them in a lineup. Was that fair? Would you want that to happen to your son?

There is a big difference between identifying a man you know and identifying a man you saw for a few seconds. The government has no eyewitness who knew either of these men before. But the defense witness Nicola Gatti knew Sacco for five years. He saw the robbers from 5 feet away. And he says, "I know Sacco and it wasn't Sacco."

Mrs. Andrews made some rather unpleasant remarks about my having offered her a trip to Maine, possibly in connection with her testimony. If she interpreted something that I said to her as improper, then why didn't she tell the district attorney? Why was she silent until she was cross-examined?

But don't take my word that Mrs. Andrews lied. Remember how Mrs. Campbell and Mr. Kurlansky destroyed her credibility.

We have drifted miles away from the shooting. We have drifted on with the tide, right to the reason why these men were arrested. They were arrested because they were radicals. This is the first time in my experience as a lawyer that a race was indicted as they are in this case. Is it presumed because an Italian is an Italian that he is a murderer, or that he will shield a murderer?

These robbers exhibited themselves and that car from 9 A.M. until 3 P.M. Would Sacco, who worked in a factory right near the scene of the crime, stand near that factory and then go back to work in the factory the next morning? Now if Vanzetti pulled that job at night, or if he was masked, he might chance staying around, but would he stand around in broad daylight without a disguise? Does it make any sense?

Sacco's mother had died, and his father wrote him a letter asking him to come to Italy. Would Sacco, a family man with a wife and child and a sick father, take part in a holdup?

Would Williams lie that he had seen Sacco in Boni's Restaurant, and put himself in the newspaper where he could be marked for life as a man who helped a murderer? Would Andrower, the clerk in the Italian consulate, lie for a murderer?

And what about Hayes? He was on the train to Boston on April 15. He doesn't say he saw Sacco, but Sacco picked him out and said he saw him. Doesn't that prove that Sacco was on that train?

For his alibi, Vanzetti has only poor people, like Rosen, the Jewish fellow who sold him cloth, and Brini. So what is there against Vanzetti? Only that he happened to be alive at this time. That is all there is against Vanzetti, except that he, unmarried, and patriotic in his way, was trying to help his friends out after he got the news in New York.

Vanzetti went to New York to find out what happened to Salsedo. He went there and was advised to get rid of all the radical literature. On May 5 he went to get that literature. But a trap had been set for Boda. And when that trap was sprung, unfortunately Sacco and Vanzetti were in it. You may want to condemn these men because they are radicals, but does that prove that they killed anyone?

As for Officer Connolly, I say take him out of the case, because no other man on the streetcar heard his remarks or saw what Connolly did. If you throw his testimony out, all question of the defendants showing their guilt goes out of this case. Of course the government had to use consciousness of guilt, because their identifications will not stand the test.

Yes, these men lied and lied when they were arrested. Why? Because they were afraid they might be deported like other radicals.

Now, gentlemen, gun expert Van Amburgh testified that the No. 3 bullet that killed Berardelli came from Sacco's .32-caliber Colt. There must be some outstanding identifying thing about that gun to make him say that. Now what is that special condition? Van Amburgh says there are irregularities on bullet No. 3 caused by rust in the gun barrel. But he says this is not an unusual thing to find in Colt revolvers. Now if he had said it is an unusual thing, I would understand how he feels confident to say that this bullet came from that gun. But he did not say it was an unusual thing to find. When the users of the microscope can't agree, when experts called by both sides sharply disagree, then I take it that ordinary men such as you and I should well hesitate to take a human life.

And about Vanzetti's gun: Slater testified that he sold it to Orciani and it eventually was sold to Vanzetti. Slater recognized the gun because the enamel was off from the end of the barrel. He recognized the case because of the tear on the holster and the little strap and the brass knob.

What of Berardelli's revolver? Fitzemeyer testified that Vanzetti's gun had a new hammer. Van Amburgh looked at the hammer and said it was new. But Burns, who has spent forty years in the job, said the hammer was used. And Fitzgerald, who works for Colt, said the same thing. Fitzemeyer testified that the Berardelli revolver he repaired was a .32. Vanzetti's gun is a .38.

Yes, Sacco and Vanzetti had guns on them. Does that prove they did the Braintree murders?

Be careful in weighing the evidence. Let no prejudice be in your mind for one second. I want every one of you to treat these two defendants as if they were your own brothers. I realize the burden I am asking of you—to help men you are not in sympathy with. I am asking you the almost impossible. I thank you, gentlemen.

The Prosecution's Closing Statement

Now listen carefully to District Attorney Frederick Katzmann's closing statement for the prosecution. Remember to separate the facts from the emotional presentation, for your verdict must be based on facts, not emotions.

This crime was premeditated. These men were waiting from 9:20 A.M. until 3 P.M. to kill and rob. If that is not deliberate premeditation and an act of extreme malice, there never was and can never be a first-degree murder in Massachusetts.

We think that we have proven to you beyond any reasonable doubt that Sacco fired a bullet from his Colt and killed Berardelli. Some other person whose name we do not know killed Parmenter. That murderer was not Vanzetti. But Vanzetti was there actively aiding Sacco and the other murderer. And under the law his help and presence makes him just as guilty as Sacco.

Peter McCullum says when he raised the window and looked out from the second floor, he saw a man beside Berardelli's body with a bright nickel gun in his left hand putting a money box into the auto. I do not claim that McCullum said that the man was Sacco. We say that man was Sacco. We say that he had his own gun in his pocket and had Berardelli's gun in his left hand. Later he gave Berardelli's gun to Vanzetti.

Now what is the defense in this case? It is three-handed, gentlemen. First there are witnesses who say that neither of these men were the men other witnesses saw in the escaping car. The second part of the defense states that these two men were someplace else that day. And a third part of the defense has been to convince you that these men lied from guilt over a minor offense and not because they were guilty of murder.

What witnesses have they produced who show that neither man was in that bandit car either before, during, or after the crime? The workers at the excavation site. But once the firing started, every laborer ran away because there was no real place for them to hide because the excavation site was at street level. So how could they see the robbers?

As for Frantello's story: Remember how poorly

he described two jurymen just opposite him? Also remember that Frank Burke's description of the man next to the driver differs from any other witnesses' description of that man.

And what about these alibis? How are they put together? Corl says he remembers he saw Vanzetti on April 15 because he was painting the boat that week and because his wife's birthday fell on April 17. Rosen testified that on April 15 he sold cloth to Vanzetti, but he couldn't tell you when he visited any other towns. And you are supposed to believe him because his wife paid his poll tax that day.

And those men at Boni's restaurant remember seeing Sacco there on April 15 because at noon they were discussing a banquet to be given that night. But when they were discussing the banquet it was going on. What logic is there between any of these things that these men say helps them to pinpoint the date?

The third part of the defense tries to explain all the lies the defendants told me when they were arrested. They said that they lied because they knew they were guilty of a federal offense—distributing or having radical books. They also said they acted guilty because they had evaded the draft in 1917. Lie upon lie because they said they were afraid I would find out that they were draft evaders. But I am not a federal official. I have nothing to do with deportation.

Vanzetti had learned on April 25 in New York

that probably there would be raids on May 1 against people who had radical literature in their houses. He returned to Plymouth on April 29 and supposedly was very frightened he would be deported. But for six days, he never asked anyone to hide any literature. If this mortal dread made them tell lies, why did Sacco leave scores of radical books in his house that so scared his wife that she burned them the day after he was arrested? Their fear of being deported is their whole explanation for their guilty conduct. It is an absurd defense. There was no literature in their pockets when they were arrested, so why were they so worried?

But they had arsenals upon them. These tender men, who ran to Mexico because they did not want to shoot a fellow human being in warfare, had enough guns and ammunition to kill thirty-seven men if each shot took effect. Do men going on a social call to see a friend arm themselves this way?

Will you ever forget Vanzetti's uncontrollable outburst, "You are a liar," which burst from his lips when Connolly spoke? Vanzetti showed that same gruff voice when Reed heard him call out, "What in 'H' did you stop us for?"

That dark cap, which is the cap of the man who killed Berardelli, is Sacco's. Don't take my word for it, gentlemen. One of you who wears a 7⅛, try the cap on.

The only question is: Who did the shooting? Witness Pelser said that he had lied at first because he did not want to testify. But when he decided to come to court, he positively identified Sacco, and he was the nearest to the shooting.

And what about Harry Dolbeare? He was called as a juryman like you. He recognized Sacco and became a witness for the prosecution.

I agree with the defense that Levangie is wrong that Vanzetti was the driver, but he saw Vanzetti's face in that car. Isn't it possible that in the quick glance when Levangie saw Vanzetti, he was seated directly behind the driver, and it looked like Vanzetti was driving. Why would Levangie lie?

In lower court Mary Splaine said, "I will not positively say he is the man," but she also said, "I will not say he is not the man." On reflection she told you she was positive. Do you think this young Christian lady would lie and take a human life away? And what about Austin Reed? Why would he swear away Vanzetti's life?

And do you understand why we didn't produce Mrs. Campbell as a witness? This elderly lady testified that the man was scrunched down under the car and that she could tell it was not Sacco by his cheek.

The night the defendants were arrested, where were they? In West Bridgewater, not far from where the getaway car was found. Can you put two and two together?

Gentlemen, bullet No. 3 was fired by a Colt .32. What does Van Amburgh say identifies bullet No. 3 as being fired from Sacco's Colt? The fact that while fouling from rust is a peculiarity of any gun that is not cleaned properly after it is fired, and more or less common, the pitting on the inside of the barrel of the Sacco revolver is marked one inch in from the muzzle end at the right-hand side of the lands. Now what did Van Amburgh say would be the effect of rust pits in a barrel? He said it would cause scoring along the edge of the groove in the bullet. Look at bullet No. 3 and at the other bullets test fired through the Sacco Colt, and you will see pronounced scorings on the edge of all these bullets.

Are you satisfied with how Slater identified the gun supposedly sold to Vanzetti? And why didn't the defense bring Orciani, who supposedly sold Vanzetti the gun, into this courtroom and have him testify? Maybe Orciani's testimony would not be helpful to Vanzetti.

Fitzemeyer, a gunsmith for thirty-one years, said a new hammer was put in that gun. Who knows more about it, the man who put the hammer in or James E. Burns, an expert who never saw the gun until he came into the courtroom?

I am going back now to discuss some witnesses I have omitted. Brooks said a man got off at East Braintree with regularity, and the defense is trying to make you believe that a man who had been getting off within four to six weeks after April 15 with some regularity would have to ask where the East Braintree station was. That man knew where it was. Remember Brooks did not say he saw this man get off April 15. Faulkner picked out the defendant from a lineup with five prisoners. The defense wanted that kind of test. They have gotten it.

Back to Mrs. Andrews. The defense had the record of a typewritten statement taken during its interview with her. If she ever said to the defense that outrageously foolish statement that Kurlansky reported, you can be sure that the defense would have told us.

As for the consulate official Andrower, he saw about 200 passport applications a day. He says that April 15 was a very slow day. Possibly he remembers Sacco's large picture, but the way that he ties it up to that all-important date of April 15 is because he was laughing and happened to look at a calendar pad on a desk. Is laughing so unusual to him that he remembers it thirteen months later?

Gentlemen, a jury must decide the facts carefully. Leave aside any sympathy for Mrs. Berardelli and Mrs. Parmenter. Leave any sympathy for Mrs. Sacco and her children out of this case. Gentlemen, do your duty. Do it like men.

The Judge's Charge

After the lawyers finished their closing statements, Judge Thayer talked to the jury. He *charged* (instructed) the jurors with the law. He explained how the law applied to the case, and how they must follow it in reaching their verdict. A judge's charge is supposed to be impartial, favoring neither one side nor the other.

On that day there were three large vases of flowers on Judge Thayer's desk. They were congratulatory bouquets for his birthday. Thayer moved one vase over to the right to have a full view of every juror and began his charge.

Mr. Foreman and Gentlemen of the jury, you were called to render a most important service. And though you knew the service would be hard, painful, and tiresome, like the true soldier, you responded in the spirit of supreme American loyalty. Loyalty to God and to country is the highest and noblest type of American citizenship. Let your eyes be blinded to every ray of sympathy or prejudice, but let them receive the beautiful sunshine of the truth of reason. I beg you not to allow the fact that the defendants are Italian to influence or prejudice you.

The prosecution must establish beyond a reasonable doubt that these defendants were two of the five robbers. The identity of the defendants is one of the important facts for you to determine.

How are you going to do this? Think about the witnesses—their power of vision, their freedom from nervous strain or excitement, their bias, and the length of their observation. The most important qualification of a witness to tell us what he saw depends upon his intellectual keenness.

The question of what gun the fatal bullet came from is very important. The gun experts on both sides disagree. The prosecution claims that Berardelli's gun was found on Vanzetti. If that is true, he must have been at the shooting. So you see that the new hammer is very important in identifying this gun. Again the experts disagree on this.

The prosecution also says that a cap found near Berardelli's body was Sacco's. But Sacco says that that cap never belonged to him. You must decide if it did.

The law says that intentional lies and concealing truth show consciousness of guilt and can be used against a defendant, but only when this relates to the charges. The defendants admit that they lied. Did they lie to remove suspicion that they were involved in the murders? If they did, then such lies show their consciousness of guilt. Or did they lie to protect themselves and their friends from being deported or arrested because they were radicals and had radical books? If that is true, then these lies do not show consciousness of guilt about the murders.

What actually took place at the time of the arrest? Is Officer Connolly's testimony that Vanzetti put his hand in his hip pocket to use his gun true? The defendants swore that nothing like that happened. If Vanzetti intended to use his gun, that tends to prove consciousness of guilt of some crime. But Vanzetti denies making those moves. You must decide what is the truth.

Finally, you must consider the alibis. The defendants state they were somewhere else when the crimes were committed and therefore could not have committed them.

You must determine the facts. Enter the jury room and reflect long and well.

Be the Jury

The jury began deliberating at 2:55 P.M. They probably discussed the following questions:

Has the prosecutor proved Sacco and Vanzetti guilty beyond a reasonable doubt?

Go over what each witness said. Did you believe the witness? Did the cross-examination prove that the testimony was false or unreliable?

Go over what each defense witness said. Did you believe this witness? Did the cross-examination prove that the testimony was false or unreliable?

When jurors review evidence to determine facts, they may call in the court stenographer to read the record of both testimony and the lawyers' and judge's statements back to them.

At any point in your deliberations, you may turn back to clarify the testimony. Use the *Stenographer's Notes* to locate specific points.

When you have reached your verdict, turn the page to find out what the Dedham jury decided.

The Verdict

At 7:55 P.M., after five hours, the jury returned to the courtroom. The clerk asked the defendants to stand. The clerk turned to the jury and asked, "Gentlemen of the jury, have you agreed upon your verdict?"

"Yes, we have," said the foreman. He returned the paper with the verdict to the clerk.

"Mr. Foreman, hold up your right hand and look upon the prisoner, Sacco. Prisoner, look upon the foreman. What say you, Mr. Foreman, is Nicola Sacco guilty or not guilty of murder in the first degree?"

"Guilty."

The clerk questioned the foreman: "What say you, Mr. Foreman, is Bartolomeo Vanzetti guilty or not guilty of murder in the first degree?"

"Guilty."

Vanzetti was silent. Sacco cried out, *"Sono in-nocente! Sono innocente!* [I am innocent! I am in-nocent!]"

His wife ran toward him and threw her arms around his neck. "What am I going to do?" she cried out. "They kill my man." Sacco stroked her head and spoke softly to her. A police officer led her back to her seat.

As the jury walked out of the courtroom, Sacco cried out, "They kill an innocent man!" The defendants were taken back to jail.

SACCO AND VANZETTI ARE FOUND GUILTY OF FIRST DEGREE MURDER

Headline from *The Boston Herald*

Guilty or Innocent?

This case is still being analyzed. Many people feel that Sacco and Vanzetti did not get a fair trial because in 1921, immigrants or people with radical political ideas were considered dangerous. Some people think that the jury could not believe that they lied because they feared they had been arrested because of their political beliefs. The prosecutor's questioning of Sacco about his love for America and his draft evasion is seen as vicious, its only purpose to convince the jury that Sacco was unpatriotic and unloving of a country that welcomed immigrants.

Many witnesses said that Vanzetti was in

Plymouth on April 15. Many eyewitnesses said that neither defendant was at the shooting. But most of these witnesses were Italians or Spaniards. Many spoke little or poor English and used interpreters. Some people think that the jury did not value their testimony as much as the testimony of Splaine and Reed.

Some people feel that Judge Thayer was not fair. They say he should have stopped the prosecutor from questioning Sacco about his political views, because they did not relate to the case and prejudiced the jury. Some critics feel that in Thayer's charge, references to loyalty to God and country reflected negatively on the defendants. Thayer's statement that the best quality for an eyewitness was intellect is seen as a direct slur on those defense witnesses who required interpreters. In those times, even more so than today, speaking English was looked upon as a sign of intelligence.

A diary kept by juror John Dever reveals that the jurors decided within an hour that Sacco and Vanzetti were guilty, but felt it wouldn't look right to leave the jury room so quickly, so they stayed there for five hours. Interviewed years later, some jurors denied that prejudice had anything to do with the verdicts.

Be the Judge

Sacco and Vanzetti's supporters did not give up trying to free the men. Protests against the convictions were held in the United States and Europe. Over the next six years the defense made several motions for a new trial. To get a new trial, lawyers must show that something happened during the trial that violated the defendants' rights or they must produce new evidence that would have affected the verdict.

Now step into the judge's chambers and BE THE JUDGE.

The Appeals for a New Trial

Read the *affidavits* (sworn written statements by witnesses) and decide if the defendants should get a new trial. You need accept only *one* motion to give them a new trial.

Defense Motion No. 1: Ripley-Daly Motion

The law says that jurors may not consider anything not admitted as evidence. However, Vanzetti's lawyer, McAnarney, described a talk he had with Walter Ripley, the foreman of the jury. This talk showed that during the trial, some jurors had seen "evidence" in the form of bullets similar to those in Vanzetti's gun. The defense argued that this violated the law.

McAnarney Affidavit:

A month after the trial, I met Ripley. He said that he had shown three .38-caliber bullets, similar to Vanzetti's bullets, to other jurors. He had put one of his bullets into Vanzetti's gun. Some jurors put marks on Ripley's bullets to distinguish them from the Vanzetti bullets. The jurors talked about these bullets. Ripley died three days after our talk, before I had a chance to get an affidavit from him.

Mrs. Ripley testified that she had found two .38-caliber bullets in the pocket of the vest worn by her husband while he was a juror. Two jurors signed affidavits saying that they had seen Ripley's bullets. Two jurors said they had heard about his bullets but they hadn't seen them. None of the jurors remembered what was said about the bullets.

The defense argued that Walter Daly's affidavit showed that Ripley was not an impartial juror as required under the Sixth Amendment.

Daly Affidavit:

Before the trial, I met Ripley. He told me he was going to be on the Sacco-Vanzetti trial. I said I thought they were innocent. It wasn't reasonable to suppose a man would rob a factory where he was well known in broad daylight. Ripley replied, "Damn them, they ought to hang anyways!"

Be the Judge

Could the jurors keep an open mind after seeing the bullets and drawing their own opinions about them?

Does Ripley's statement show prejudice against the defendants?

Defense Motion No. 2: Gould-Pelser Motion

Roy Gould did not testify at the trial because the defense did not track him down until October 1921. The defense insisted that Gould's testimony was new because he was closer to the getaway car than any other witness and that his testimony would have resulted in a different verdict.

Gould Affidavit:

I was 5 to 10 feet away from the Buick as it went up Pearl Street. I had a clear view of the man on the front seat to the right of the driver. That man fired at me and put a hole through my coat. That man was about 25 years old. He was dark complected with a slight build and clean-cut features. He wore a blue suit with a small chain across the vest. Black hair stuck out from his cap. I have seen Sacco in prison. He wasn't one of the bandits.

Pelser changed his testimony and said that Sacco was not one of the robbers.

Pelser Affidavit:

I only glimpsed the man with the gun. I was too scared to notice anything. I did not see the robbers clearly enough to identify them. I told this to the prosecutor.

But two days after signing the affidavit, Pelser signed a counteraffidavit in which he stated that Sacco's lawyer had persuaded him to change his testimony.

Pelser Counteraffidavit:

I was drinking pretty heavy on Saturday when a man called for me in regards to the Sacco case. He did not say which side he represented. He said he wanted to show me a couple of pictures. He gave me some money and bought me dinner and cigarettes. We went into some office. He introduced me to Mr. Moore, Sacco's lawyer. Mr. Moore locked the door. He patted me on the back and gave me a cigar and talked to me about the Sacco case. He had three or four men in the office and a girl stenographer. He asked me one question and another and finally my whole story contradicted what I had said in court. When I came to my senses the next day, I called the prosecutor.

Prosecutors Katzmann and Williams also submitted affidavits. They denied putting any pressure on Pelser to testify that the man he had seen was Sacco.

Be the Judge

Would Gould's testimony have swayed the jurors and changed the verdict?

When did Pelser tell the truth: in the affidavit or the counteraffidavit?

Should Pelser's original trial testimony be thrown out?

Defense Motion No 3: Andrews Motion

Lola Andrews took back her identification of Sacco. The defense claimed her testimony should not have been considered by the jury.

Andrews Affidavit:

When I saw Sacco in the county jail, two officers asked me if he was the robber I had seen. I said I didn't know. The officers repeatedly said, "You know he is the man you saw." Their manner made me think I had better say that Sacco was the man. Later I told the Assistant District Attorney that I could not positively identify Sacco. He shook his finger in my face and said, "You can put it stronger than that. I know you can." His loud voice was commanding and intimidating. I felt confused and uncertain. So I lied and said I had seen Sacco.

After I testified at the trial, I told the same two officers that they had gotten me into a nice mess, and that I didn't want to go back to be cross-examined. They said, "You have got to go back. If you don't, the government will release facts about your private life."

It is absolutely false that the defense ever offered me any kind of trip to Maine.

Shortly after Andrews signed the affidavit, she signed a counteraffidavit that the defense had pressured her into taking back her testimony.

Andrews Counteraffidavit:

Without my permission, my nineteen-year-old son was brought to Boston to meet with me and Moore and his two assistants. One of his assistants told me that I was telling a terrible lie about Sacco and should clear my conscience of it. The other one said my boy had come here because he knew I had told the lie and it was going to hurt him through his life. I started crying. They told me it was time to undo what I had done. They said they had sworn statements from twelve people that I had a bad reputation. Moore said no one would see these statements, not even my son, if I said I did not recognize Sacco. I said I could not do that. Moore gave me a paper and told me to sign it. They dipped the pen in the ink and put it into my hand. I was crying and asking them not to force me to sign it. My son said, "I want you to sign it. It means a lot to me." I do not remember much what happened after that, only that my boy put his arm around me and told me to sign it and have an end to this trouble.

Both prosecutors and the two police officers swore affidavits denying that they had pressured Andrews in any way.

Moore and his assistants swore affidavits denying Andrews' charges in her counteraffidavit.

Be the Judge

Is Andrews telling the truth in the affidavit or the counteraffidavit?

Defense Motion No. 4: Hamilton-Proctor Motion

Two ballistics experts, Dr. Alexander Hamilton and Dr. August Gill, offered new reasons to show that the fatal bullet was not fired from Sacco's gun.

Hamilton Affidavit:

I used a Bausch & Lomb compound microscope and was able to pinpoint differences between the markings on the test bullets from Sacco's pistol and the markings on bullet No. 3. According to my measurements, the land-and-groove widths in the barrel of Sacco's Colt agreed with the land-and-groove widths on the test bullets but not with the mortal bullet. I also saw from the difference in the grooves that bullet No. 3 was not made at the same time as the bullets found on Sacco.

Gill Affidavit:

I am convinced from my measurements that bullet No. 3 never passed through Sacco's gun. As for Vanzetti's revolver, it did not have a new hammer, because an essential screw did not show marks of having been removed and a new one inserted.

William Proctor swore that the prosecutor's questions were designed to mislead the jury from his real opinion. Proctor died before his affidavit went before the judge.

Proctor Affidavit:

At the trial neither the prosecutor nor the defense asked me whether I had found any evidence that bullet No. 3 had passed through Sacco's pistol. The prosecutor wanted to ask me that question but he knew what I would say and framed his question accordingly. Had I been asked directly whether I had found any evidence that bullet No. 3 had passed through Sacco's pistol, I should have answered then, as I do now, "No."

Both prosecutors submitted counteraffidavits denying Proctor's statement. They swore that Proctor had helped frame the questions asked of him in court. They suggested that perhaps Proctor had changed his testimony because the government had refused to approve his fee of $500 for his expert testimony.

The prosecution asked Van Amburgh to run new tests. These tests convinced him even more that Sacco's gun had fired the fatal bullet.

Van Amburgh Affidavit:

I used a more powerful microscope and had more photographs taken of bullet No. 3 and one test bullet. I am positive that the mortal bullet was fired in the Sacco pistol. My findings have been confirmed by Merton Robinson, a ballistics engineer for the Winchester Arms Company.

As for Dr. Gill's statements that the hammer in Vanzetti's gun had not been replaced: An expert repairman could have removed the old screw and inserted a new one without leaving any marks.

Be the Judge

If Proctor had said that the fatal bullet did not come from Sacco's gun, would that have changed the verdict?

Which gun experts are right?

Be the Judge

Now that you have read the appeals you must decide if the defendants should be given a new trial. Remember you need accept only one motion to grant them a new trial. Read over each motion. Think about each motion. If you want to refresh your memory about what some of these people said at the trial, you may use the *Stenographer's Notes* to locate their trial testimony.

Then decide:

• Did any of these four motions provide new evidence?

• Would any of this new evidence have affected the jury's verdict?

• Did any of these motions show that the defendants' rights under the Constitution were violated?

Read carefully, for if Sacco and Vanzetti do not get a new trial they may be executed.

When you have reached a decision, turn the page and find out what Judge Thayer decided.

Judge Thayer's Decisions

On the Ripley-Day Motion:

Ripley did show a few jurors three bullets and the jurors talked about them. But none of the jurors remember what that talk was, when it was, or whether it was favorable or unfavorable to the defendants. So I fail to see how this talk could or might have created any disturbing or prejudicial influence.

McAnarney talked with Ripley soon after the trial. But his affidavit was not sworn until after Ripley was dead. I believe this is significant. If Ripley's statements were important, why wasn't an affidavit prepared for his signature during his lifetime, especially when the defendants had been found guilty?

On the Gould-Pelser Motion:

This evidence only means one more eyewitness to the robbers, one more piece of the same kind of evidence. I believe this evidence would have had no effect whatever on the verdict. These verdicts did not rest on eyewitness testimony, since the defense produced more eyewitnesses to clear the defendants than the prosecution produced to incriminate them. Circumstantial evidence and evidence about consciousness of guilt are what convicted them.

Pelser's retraction is not at all trustworthy since

he was drunk at the time and withdrew his statement two days later. The prosecutors denied influencing Pelser's testimony and I believe them.

On the Andrews Motion:

It is unpleasant to pass judgment on unprofessional conduct by lawyers, but I believe that Mr. Moore is guilty of unprofessional conduct. He seems to feel that an enthusiastic belief in a client's innocence justifies any means to accomplish the ends. I believe Andrews signed her affidavit because she was intimidated.

On the Hamilton-Proctor Motion:

I criticize Proctor for charging the prosecutors with misconduct, which assails their honor and their integrity. I believe Proctor meant what he said in court and that the jury understood what he meant.

I do not believe any of these motions are sufficient grounds for a new trial.

What Happened to Sacco and Vanzetti?

Sacco and Vanzetti's supporters did not give up. In January 1926 their lawyers appealed to the Massachusetts Supreme Judicial Court. They argued that the conviction was unjust: Thayer had abused the law in allowing cross-examination of Sacco that was unrelated to the charges and that prejudiced the jury against him. The appeal also argued that the four motions required a new trial. The court upheld Thayer.

Protests against the unfairness of the trial grew. Demonstrations, letters to the editor, and telegrams to public officials increased. Celestino Medeiros, a convicted felon, confessed to being involved in the Dedham robbery. In September 1926 the defense asked Judge Thayer to let Medeiros testify in court and to set aside Sacco's conviction because of the confession. Thayer overruled both requests. He said that setting aside a jury verdict affirmed by the Massachusetts Supreme Court on the affidavit of a criminal would be a "mockery of justice and the truth."

In January 1927 the defense appealed Thayer's denial of the Medeiros motion to the

Massachusetts Supreme Court. The court again upheld Thayer.

On April 9, 1927, Thayer sentenced both men to death by electrocution. Many important Americans pressed Governor Fuller of Massachusetts to appoint a commission to review the trial. The commission reviewed the case and interviewed selected witnesses; the governor carried out a separate investigation. Amid new defense evidence was the fact that the lining in the supposed Sacco cap had been torn by a policeman, not by hanging on a nail in Sacco's factory. The defense argued that the evidence of the cap from the trial was now proven false. This alone was sufficient for a new trial.

In August the commission and the governor

concluded that the trial was fair and the two men were guilty beyond a reasonable doubt. Protests continued in the United States and throughout Europe, but on August 22, 1927, Sacco and Vanzetti were electrocuted.

Headline from *The Boston Herald*

In 1977, Massachusetts Governor Michael Dukakis signed a proclamation declaring August 22 to be "Nicola Sacco and Bartolomeo Vanzetti Memorial Day." Dukakis did not state whether he thought the men were guilty or innocent but he did say he wanted to remove "any stigma or disgrace" from their families and from the Commonwealth of Massachusetts.

What If ?

What If Sacco and Vanzetti Had Been Tried Today?

If the defendants had been tried today, questions asked in the jail without lawyers being present would not have been permitted as evidence in the court. And so this part of "consciousness of guilt" would not have been heard by the jury.

When the police show an accused person singly to a witness, the underlying message to the witness is that the police suspect the person is guilty. As a result, witnesses often falsely identify the person shown to them. Today accused persons are put in a lineup for identification. Sacco and Vanzetti were never seen in a lineup. Today all accused persons are entitled to have lawyers represent them at the time of a lineup.

In addition, if Sacco and Vanzetti had been tried today, the question of motive might have been discussed more thoroughly. In 1921, it was never shown that Sacco and Vanzetti needed to rob the guards for the money, or had a reason to kill them.

What Do You Think?

Does prejudice ever influence a juror's verdict?

Considering the controversy surrounding this case, should Sacco and Vanzetti have been executed?

Author's Note

The testimony in this book was edited from the transcript of the trial. The descriptions of people and interactions in the courtroom were taken from newspaper articles. At the original trial Sacco's lawyer, Fred Moore, and Vanzetti's lawyer, Jeremiah McAnarney, each made separate closing statements. In this book their speeches were edited and combined as one. For purposes of space, questions and answers were often combined. Not all witness evidence was included in this book nor were all the days of the trial. But the most important facts and contradictions have been included to give a balanced picture so that you could be a fair judge and fair juror.

Acknowledgments

Alan Levine, Associate Professor, Hofstra Unviversity School of Law, critiqued this book, bringing to it the seriousnesss of purpose that has marked his lifelong commitment to providing legal protection for all Americans. Fralin Agron, Kenton Kirby, Jennifer Macagnone, Sahory Montilla, Diana Ravagnan, and Rachael Sherry of Elaine Shapiro's fifth grade class at P.S. 199 in New York City brought their expertise to reading and critiquing this book. The New York Public Library provided space in the Wertheim Study to facilitate my research, and the library staff proved tireless in answering all requests. Roberta Zonghi and Giuseppe Bisaccia of the Rare Book Room in the Boston Public Library led me to important pictorial material. Michele Drohan dug up other essential photographs and newspaper clippings; Christine Kettner tolerated my intrusion on her graphic design skills; Renee Cafiero reminded me of the importance of clarity in language. Katherine Brown Tegen, as always, supported my vision, demanded revision, and tolerated my innumerable bothersome requests.

Bibliography

Ehrmann, Herbert B. *The Case That Will Not Die.* Boston: Little, Brown, 1969.

Feuerlicht, Robert. *Justice Crucified.* New York: McGraw-Hill, 1977.

Fraenkel, Osmond K. *Sacco-Vanzetti Case.* New York: Knopf, 1931.

Frankfurter, Felix. *The Case of Sacco and Vanzetti: A Critical Analysis for the Layman.* Boston: Little, Brown, 1927.

Musmanno, Michael. *After Twelve Years.* New York and London: Knopf, 1939.

Russell, Francis. *Tragedy in Dedham: The Story of the Sacco-Vanzetti Case.* New York: McGraw-Hill, 1971.

————. *Sacco and Vanzetti: The Case Resolved.* New York: Harper & Row, 1986.

Transcript of the Record of the Trial of Nicola Sacco and Bartolomeo Vanzetti in the Courts of Massachusetts and Subsequent Proceedings 1920–27. Mamaroneck, N.Y.: Appeal, 1969.

Newspapers consulted were the Boston *Daily Globe*, the Boston *Evening Transcript*, *The Boston Herald*, and the Boston *Post*.

Stenographer's Notes

These notes cover only testimony accepted at the trial because that is all you, as jury members, are allowed to see.

Page numbers in *italics* refer to illustrations.

selection of, 26–29

Katzmann, Frederick, *24*
  closing statement of, 130–36
Kelley, George, 121
Kurlansky, Harry, 55, 92–93,
  126, 136

Levangie, Michael, 31–33,
  56–57, 125, 134
  position as eyewitness, *32*
lies
  by defendants, 64, 108, 128,
    132–33, 139
  by Sacco, 115, 119–21
  by Vanzetti, 113–14
  by Louis Pelser, 50–51

McAnarney, Jeremiah, *24*, 27
McCullum, Peter, 84–85, 131
  position as eyewitness, *82*
McNaught, Henry, 89
Matfield Crossing, 33, 62–63
means to commit crime, 38
medical experts, 40
men seen in crime area, 31, 52,
  80–81, 90–91
Moore, Fred, *24*, 27
  closing statement of, 123–29
motive, 38
murderers. *See* gunmen
murders, eyewitness testimony
  about, 41–42, 44, 49–51

Neal, Shelly A., 30, 40–41, 124
  position as eyewitness, *32*
New York, Vanzetti's visit to,
  127

objections
  by defense, 68, 117, 118
  by prosecution, 108
occupants of getaway car, 31–33,
  41, 46–48, 78–79, 83–84,
  86–87
opening statements
  of defense, 75–76
  of prosecution, 30–34
opportunity to commit crime,
  38
Orciani, Riccardo, 33, 103, 129,
  135

Parmenter, Frederick, 30–31,
  40, 41–42, 130
passport picture of Sacco, 102,
  136
Pelser, Louis, 49–51, 84–85, 134
  position as eyewitness, *32*
Pierce, Winfred, 76, 83–84
  position as eyewitness, *82*
Plymouth, Vanzetti seen in, 76,
  98–99
police
  testimony of, 128, 139
  treatment of defendants by,
    109–11, 112
  at trial, 25–26, 29
politics of defendants, 127–28
  of Sacco, 119
Pratt, Ernest, 89
preliminary hearings, testimony
  from, 45, 47
premeditation, 38, 58–59, 60,
  130
prison, treatment of defendants
  in, 110–11

Doreen Rappaport

is the author of many books for children, including LIVING DANGEROUSLY: *American Women Who Risked Their Lives for Adventure*; ESCAPE FROM SLAVERY: *Five Journeys to Freedom*; THE BOSTON COFFEE PARTY; TROUBLE AT THE MINES, an Honor Book for the 1988 Jane Addams Children's Book Award; and AMERICAN WOMEN: *Their Lives in Their Words*, a 1990 Notable Children's Trade Book in the Field of Social Studies and a 1992 ALA Best Book for Young Adults. THE LIZZIE BORDEN TRIAL is another title in Ms. Rappaport's BE THE JUDGE • BE THE JURY™ series.

Ms. Rappaport is also the creator of award-winning educational programs focusing on American history, literature, and music. She lives in New York City.